Advance Praise for Being Generous

"Ted Malloch makes a convincing and fascinating argument that humans are hard-wired for generosity, and that for both individuals and society, it is truly more blessed to give than to receive."

—Cherie Harder, president, The Trinity Forum

"We need compelling arguments that all of us are called to imitate God's generosity. This book offers such arguments and helps its readers build 'a bridge from self-centeredness to generosity.'"

—Miroslav Volf, Henry B. Wright Professor of Theology, Yale University, and founding director of the Yale Center for Faith and Culture; author of *Free of Charge: Giving and Forgiving in a Culture Stripped of Grace*

"Dr. Malloch draws on ancient wisdom and modern science to resurrect the neglected virtue of generosity. . . . This lively book will nudge many of us away from the inertia of selfishness. . . . From Oprah to Bill Gates, many have discovered the joy of being generous. Many more will as a result of this timely book."

—Paul Zak, professor of neuroeconomics, Claremont University

"Ted Malloch does a beautiful job of weaving together theory and narrative, exhortation, and science on generosity. Bravo!"

—Stephen G. Post, PhD, director, Center for Medical Humanities, Compassionate Care, and Bioethics, Stony Brook University, and president, Institute for Research on Unlimited Love

"Wise people take time to think. In this book Theodore Malloch invites us to listen in as he reflects publicly on generosity as both a religious virtue and a philanthropic practice. In his musings he explores the religious underpinnings of generosity as exemplified in the world's great religious traditions. The upshot is a book captivating and informative in its perusal of history, theology, economics, sociology, and philanthropic practice."

—Bill Enright, director, The Lake Institute on Faith & Giving, The Center on Philanthropy at Indiana University

"[*Being Generous*] explores the inner life animating the current wave of generosity, tracing the flow of grace from soul to community to world."

—Paul Schervish, director, Center on Wealth and Philanthropy, Boston College

"We need this book. Not only does Ted Malloch hold up for us wonderful past models of generosity—he also shows us how a generous spirit is crucial for human flourishing."

—Richard Mouw, president and professor of Christian philosophy, Fuller Theological Seminary

"Theodore Roosevelt Malloch offers a valuable look at the history, intent, and spirit of giving, and he advances a powerful idea: giving is not only natural, but also a fundamental part of moral health. Malloch contributes generously to the pursuit of a civil society. This book is a rewarding read for those who invest themselves in advancing the common good."

—Brian Gallagher, president and CEO, United Way

"The Salvation Army's partnership with both private and public philanthropy continue to bring comfort to the needy, while the proclamation of God's redemptive love offers individuals and communities the opportunity to enjoy a better life on earth and a place in Christ's everlasting Kingdom. *Being Generous* articulates the American relationship to charitable giving in a most powerful way."

—Israel Gaither, national commander,
The Salvation Army

"Ted Malloch develops with great sensibility and clarity the spiritual, psychological, and social roots of generosity. This argument is both compelling and inspiring. It, simply put, will make you a better person."

—Joseph Johnston Jr., retired partner,
Drinker, Biddle Reath LLP

"In reading and then practicing this book you will understand what generous virtue is—justice and fair dealing—as it leads to true happiness. I pray that the Lord will look kindly on this great gift, presented by his faithful servant."

—Pere Nicolas Buttet, moderator and spiritual director,
Fraternite Eucharistein, Switzerland

"Ted Malloch tackles a critical issue for our time—philanthropy. Young people instinctively know today that we are to have compassion for others and serve our communities. Ted gives voice to the 'why' generosity is important. He also draws on a wealth of understanding."

—Chuck Stetson, chairman, Essentials in Education

"We discover peace through (and in) the realization that the whole of existence is reflected in the parts, and from the parts comes the ever-greater whole. What Ted Malloch has done with the understanding of 'gift' rooted in human generosity is help us discover that the whole world needs the whole world."

—Abdul Aziz Said, Mohammed Said Farsi Chair of Islamic Peace, School of International Service, American University

"Malloch is absolutely right that generosity is a critical virtue for human flourishing. . . . Faith-based contributions to civil society are indeed rooted in what he forcefully describes and here advocates!"

—Jay Hein, former director of the White House Office of Faith-Based and Community Initiatives

"Finally a book that makes the principles of biblical generosity relevant for the 21st century! This is a new Bible."

—H. Skip Weitzen, author, Hypergrowth

"We need to see ourselves, first and foremost, as receivers—grateful, joyful recipients of Christ's grace—and only secondly as givers. I know this book can serve you on your journey of generosity. . . . Read it and become an increasingly generous giver."

—Todd Harper, executive vice president, Generous Giving

Being Generous

All royalties from the sale of this book will go to GlobalGiving. GlobalGiving's online marketplace allows donors to find and fund (IRS tax deductible) grass-roots projects that appeal to their specific interests. GlobalGiving offers projects in more than one hundred countries featuring a variety of initiatives ranging from education and health care to economic development and the environment. www.globalgiving.com

Being Generous

Theodore Roosevelt Malloch

TEMPLETON PRESS

Templeton Press
300 Conshohocken State Road, Suite 550
West Conshohocken, PA 19428
www.templetonpress.org

Unless otherwise indicated, all scripture references are from
the King James Version (KJV).

Typeset and designed by Gopa and Ted2, Inc.

Library of Congress Cataloging-in-Publication Data

Malloch, Theodore R.
  Being generous / Theodore Roosevelt Malloch.
    p. cm.
  ISBN-13: 978-1-59947-316-1 (alk. paper)
  ISBN-10: 1-59947-316-X (alk. paper)
  1. Generosity. I. Title.
  BJ1533.G4.M34 2009
  177'.7—dc22

                                    2009010013

Printed in the United States of America

09 10 11 12 13 14   10 9 8 7 6 5 4 3 2 1

For
everyone who struggles to be more
generous—the world over

"Aeternitas vitae resonat tamquam imago"

Contents

Foreword

MY DEAR FATHER, the successful investor John Templeton, taught me that optimism and gratitude go hand in
hand. During an interview on the Canadian television program *Cross Currents*, he once said of his philanthropy that
he did not inherit his wealth, but that at the time of his
marriage to my mother, Judith Folk, they pledged to commit half of their income to charity and investment. This led
to a game of bargain hunting, budget control, and careful
investment, which taken together provided the foundation
for his wealth. Coupled with a lifestyle of thrift and sav-
ing was a desire he had been given from early childhood
simply to help others. He suggested that this willingness
to be helpful and useful was actually a source of his optimism, just as optimism was a basis for being helpful and
useful. As he said, "The two go hand in hand." And then
he added some thoughts about the connection between
gratitude and being generous, which is the subject of this
thoughtful and timely book.

"Thanksgiving and gratitude will revolutionize your

life. If you wake up every day and think of five new things that you are overwhelmingly grateful for, your day will go better, people will like you better, you'll be more successful. Try it!" A little girl said to my father once, "I can't think of anything to be thankful for." So he said, "Just stop breathing for three minutes and you'll be very thankful you can breathe again."

Optimism and thankfulness certainly characterized my late father's career, and I have also tried to live by these ideals. But they have always been accompanied by serious attention to in-depth study and thorough preparation. "Is it cost-effective?" was always one of Dad's favorite responses to almost any question. The link between thrift and generosity, as well as the joy that was experienced by the giver as a side effect of his or her gifts are things I too have thought about deeply and strive to practice. I commend it to you.

John Wesley, the founder of Methodism, perhaps said it as well as it has ever been said when he suggested the proverb: "Make all you can; save all you can; give all you can." The true measure of persons is not what they own or have consumed, but rather what they have given to others— in time, treasure, and talent. At the end of his own life, Wesley had very few physical possessions: just one worn coat and two silver spoons. He had given away all of his wealth to advance the kingdom. Thrift and generosity do go together and are greater than the sum of their parts. I have said many times that practicing these virtues in tandem will greatly affect any human life. I am also convinced that as we find ways of being generous, as suggested in this book, we will move closer to the goal of discovering and experiencing true joy. The Talmud puts it most forcefully: "Deeds of giving are the equivalent to the entirety of God's commandments."

I often read the Psalms for inspiration and energy, something I recommend to everyone. The songs and poetry of King David are full of wisdom. No piece of wisdom is more insightful than that found in Psalm 112:5: "Good will come to him who is generous and lends freely, who conducts his affairs with justice" (NIV).

I have for some time harbored a disturbing fear that many children growing up today in our materialist culture feel entitled to nearly everything. They can't live without this or that, the latest gizmo or fastest device. They never seem to have enough. We need to teach our children how to live, how to save, and why one should give. Children need to know what is truly important in life. They need to know that money can't buy everything.

I worry most that we are not teaching our children at the earliest age to be generous. My father taught me that, as he often said, "The more love you give, the more you have left." He also taught, "Love given grows, love hoarded dwindles." In fact, he made this one of his key "Laws of Life." He not only preached these words, but practiced them as well.

In my medical practice, I frequently interacted with patients experiencing times of severe hurt and suffering. Many faced life-and-death issues head on. Often what amazed me most about the healing process was how those who were most generous seemed to heal faster, better, and with greater endurance than others. There is a natural— I would even say God-given—quality to generosity that transforms individuals and everything they touch, including their relationships, forever.

I still dream of a world in which generosity becomes an essential value—a routine part of life—where giving to others is a welcomed opportunity, not a burden or an obligation. I have this dream not only for our great country and its peoples but also for the entire world.

John M. Templeton Jr., MD

Preface

MUCH OF WHAT I have written here is neither new nor original. The packaging or combination of the elements is distinct, but the thinking has existed in parts—bits and pieces, jumbled elements—for nearly centuries. This work synthesizes many current convergent streams of thought and practice. It represents a lifetime of reflection and study, of questioning and then forging ahead. My goal is first to persuade, and then to guide readers toward a life of greater giving.

I am blessed to have a firm foundation on which to build my argument. I had parents who taught me how to give and who themselves gave sacrificially based on their confessed convictions. In my family, giving was not an option, but a formal habit. However, it never came easily to me. I have always had a "meritocratic" outlook. That is, I instinctively lean toward the view that you get what you earn, what you deserve. Thereafter—and only thereafter—is it "yours," all yours, to keep, spend, loan, or invest.

I found it hard—often very hard—to give what I had earned away. I grew up in the "me generation." Like Narcissus gazing into the pool and seeing his own reflection,

I, along with many of my contemporaries, was too self-centered to focus on "the other." Thus, I had to relearn much of what the culture taught me. I had to practice religious disciplines in order to become more generous. This is something I still must work at constantly, for ultimately the business of giving is unfinished business.

At the same time, the generosity I have been fortunate enough to witness has influenced who I have become and who I want to be. My wife and four children have given more to me than can ever be accounted, and for me the greatest part is the sheer joy of nurturing them—seeing them mature so as to find their way in the world. I in turn have given to them, as is expected of a husband and father. But such instinctive giving is rooted not so much in generosity as it is in the natural shape of family life, life that is shared. True giving, as I describe herein, is rooted not in reciprocity but in compassion. This being the case, it always attempts to match the gift with the need. Indeed, the most basic truth about generosity is that it's about meeting the needs (emotional, financial, and physical) of others. This process results in the giver, in turn, being richly blessed. This explains why people who give often say, "I got back more than I ever gave."

Nevertheless, too many people have yet to start giving. Either they are plain stingy or they are too self-centered, too self-contained. Regardless, their habit injures not just human relationships, but also the soul. Their selfishness renders them incapable of being "surprised by joy," to use Wordsworth's phrase.

Many friends, mentors, and colleagues have helped to shape my thinking and to push me onward. They have given much, and I record the debt here. I cannot thank them individually, as there are too many to list. But to thank them collectively is in no way to diminish their gifts to me. The Templeton Foundation deserves a special word of gratitude for funding this project and helping me to launch the Spiritual Enterprise Institute under whose auspices this book was conceived and written. Kimon Sargeant, Charles Harper, Arthur Schwartz, and Barnaby Marsh have been my allies in this work. Susan Arellano, the publisher of Templeton Press, and her editors did a fabulous job creating the theme and campaign for this effort. I am especially grateful to the late Sir John Templeton for challenging me to undertake this charge. His generosity—and that of his son Jack—has made this work and so much else possible. I am grateful that father and son alike were and are known for living what they profess.

My only attestation in life is like that of St. Augustine, *"Ego in hoc notus sum, et ad hoc veni ut veritatem attesti."*

I would now add, "Discover what being generous means, and begin living it."

Theodore Roosevelt Malloch

Jupiter Island, Florida

2008

Introduction

Think of giving not as a duty but as a privilege.

JOHN D. ROCKEFELLER

In 1995, MIT Media Lab's Nicholas Negroponte wrote a best-selling book with the audacious title *Being Digital*.[1] The book was in essence a nonfiction science and technology forecast describing a world free of wires. An instant classic, in many ways it came to define the Internet era. *Being Digital* provided a general history of several digital media technologies, many of which Negroponte himself was directly involved in developing in the labs. He analyzed the advantages and disadvantages of the new technologies and tried to predict how they would evolve. He argued that humanity is inevitably headed toward a future where everything that *can* be digitalized *will* be digitalized. He was very soon proved right.

Being Digital and its thesis remind us that, as the French poet Paul Valéry once remarked, the future is not what it used to be. And this is largely because, like the future, change is not what it used to be. Negroponte's description of the growth of digital technologies as "almost genetic in its nature" suggests an exponential expansion of the rate of change. In this sense, Negroponte's book was as much about change as it was about the future. This is hardly surprising, since it is difficult to refer to one without referring to the other. We can no longer describe the future or the process of change without addressing digital technology, since all three are facets of the same intricate process.

Similarly, I cannot address the topic of generosity without addressing people, for generosity is rooted in the things people feel and do. It is a virtue, a habit that shapes and governs a way of life. It influences expectations, causing people to look at the world as though others—not themselves—are the principal reason for the world's existence.

It is my hope that in the new world of connectedness to which we are advancing, the virtue of generosity will find fertile ground, that it will spread through the world as peace spreads through a congregation or good cheer through a carnival. Like Negroponte, I see the overthrow of the paradigms of the past. Much that is stale and out-of-date is vanishing. We are beginning to share our traditions, religions, and moral philosophies. And we appear to be ready in our increasing affluence to forge something new: a global civilization based on spiritual information.

At the core of this new way of being is the virtue of generosity. It, too, can become ubiquitous. This book is an attempt to see what being generous means and what it might entail for everyone in our common future.

I contend that the future is half inherited and half created. Nothing under the sun is ever entirely new. We need to recall the collected wisdom of the ages. The big and important questions people have addressed through the ages are still with us and are not going to go away anytime soon. The Great Books, our various religious heritages and sacred literature, and science all provide us with valuable starting points in this new journey into old uncertainties. In the context of this grand pursuit, however, it is my belief that being generous may be the most important thing we can do not just for others, but for ourselves, for our societies, for our progeny, and even for the God or gods we choose to worship.

Well over two hundred years ago, Adam Smith said more or less the same thing, albeit in the voice of the Scottish Enlightenment, in his seminal work, *The Wealth of Nations*, for which he is rightly famous. Earlier, in *The Theory of Moral Sentiments*, he wrote, "It is the best head joined to the best heart."[2] Now is the time to experience what it means to be generous and what can be gained when a global civilization makes a concerted effort to celebrate and practice this virtue.

Being Generous

Generosity: A Universal Moral Urge 1

We ourselves feel that what we are doing is just a drop in the ocean. But the ocean would be less because of that missing drop.

MOTHER TERESA OF CALCUTTA

AMPLE EVIDENCE suggests that being generous—giving selflessly to others—lies at the heart of what it means to be a thoughtful and moral human being. Through the ages, the world's cultures and great religions have in profound though different ways sought to answer the big question: *how should we live?* Part of the answer has to do with how we ought to treat others, particularly those who are most in need.

Almost all of the more than six billion inhabitants of our planet are connected to a spiritual or moral tradition that has in some way addressed the question of how we ought to live. Thus we all have some capacity to grow in our understanding of generosity as both an ethical virtue and a best practice.

I hope through the following overview to "connect the dots" around the globe and among traditions that have stood the test of time. Focusing on what these traditions have to say about generosity, my goal is not to arrive at some great interfaith boiling down of essentials, but rather to celebrate our human nature and the diverse paths we have taken toward living well in the eyes of God.

Judaism

The religion of the Jews is rooted in the story of a people, which is also the story of the world. The story shows us the beginning of the world, the laws for living in it successfully, and the final goal toward which all things progress, provided we humans behave as we should: the goal of the kingdom, the new Zion in which the good will be rewarded, and the sin of Adam redeemed. It is a story of creation, of loss, and of final redemption—and its outlines have been bequeathed to the two great successor religions, Christianity and Islam.

In Judaism, we encounter the story of a people chosen by God to be an example to the world through obedience to the divine law contained in the Torah (the first five books of the Hebrew Bible) and through conduct according to the rule of loving-kindness. From the earliest days of the Jewish faith can be found a tendency to condense the divine law into something immediately digestible, hence the Ten Commandments of Exodus, reduced to two in Leviticus and in Deuteronomy: "Love God with all thy soul and with all thy strength and with all thy mind and thy neighbor as thyself." We find this theme also in the famous response of Rabbi Hillel, a contemporary of Jesus, to a question. Said the rabbi, as recorded in the Talmud: "Whatever is hateful to you, do not do it to your neighbor; this is the whole *torah*, the rest is commentary." We see here the signs of a growing current of opinion that love of God and love of neighbor are one and the same.

The term *mitzvah* (plural *mitzvot*) in Judaism has to do with a Jew's obligations. It is a general term for something commanded, whether by law or by the less formal duty of loving-kindness, *tzedakah*, which corresponds to the Christian idea of charity, or disinterested love of neighbor. *Mitzvot* are not confined to any rigid system of law. Rather, they address a goodness of heart that puts others before self in all mutual dealings. Much of the rabbinical literature addresses *mitzvot*. Various maxims speak to how to live in a condition of obedience and love. As one Midrash states, "*Tzedakah* was slumbering, and Abraham aroused it. How did he do it? He built an inn with openings in every direction, and he would receive wayfarers."

Mitzvot and *tzedakah* are thus intimately connected. The way to lead a good life, a life pleasing to God, is to give. In fact, in Judaism the duty to give is considered so important that the recipient is obligated to give something back to others, the only stipulation being that a person should not give to the point where he himself becomes needy.

The emphasis on giving in the Jewish tradition is strongly implied by the fact that, in the *Mishneh Torah*, Maimonides ranked acts of charity, as follows, from the least to the most meritorious:

- giving and enabling the recipient to become self-reliant;
- giving when neither party knows the other's identity;
- giving when you know the recipient's identity, but he doesn't know yours;
- giving when you don't know the recipient's identity, but he knows yours;

- giving before being asked;
- giving after being asked;
- giving less than you should, but giving it happily;
- giving begrudgingly.

In Jewish tradition, the giving of the tithe (10 percent) to the Temple was expected, but the call to charity went further than the tithe. The ideal is to move beyond performing acts of kindness in order to become a person whose *essence* is kindness, someone for whom the *mitzvah* of loving-kindness has become a way of life.

Christianity

Christianity arose out of Judaism, and is in part a reaction to the formalized idea of gift contained in the idea of a tithe. Like Rabbi Hillel, Jesus rebelled against the ossified customs of the Temple. He wanted people to wake up to the reality of *tzedakah*—in other words, to replace safe routines with risk-taking love. He challenged the priorities of Jews who placed a heavier emphasis on tithing than on charity, mercy, and doing good.

Though early Christians did not tithe, they were fully committed to supporting their leaders and to giving to charitable causes. The Apostle Paul taught that apostles had the right to request financial support, though Paul himself did not exercise this right because he did not want to burden the congregation (1 Cor. 9:14–15). Early churches routinely supported widows, orphans, and other poor people (1 Tim. 5:9, Acts 2:45, Acts 6:1). Paul placed a special emphasis on supporting famished Christians in Jerusalem, asking the Corinthian Christians to take a regular collection to aid them. Prior to asking this, he reminded

The Pew Family

JOSEPH N. PEW founded Sun Oil Company and raised five children in a religious Presbyterian home on Philadelphia's Main Line. After his death in 1912, his children inherited and expanded the company. Their wealth was estimated at over $25 million by 1925. In charity the family supported Christian ideals and conservative ideas, especially private enterprise. In 1948 they created a trust foundation as a tribute to their parents. The Pew Charitable Trusts gave to local charities, small religious colleges, and Christian outreach. They had a rule never to donate to endowments. Originally keen on donor intent, The Pew Charitable Trusts remain today one of the largest charitable foundations in America.

Photo: Joseph N. Pew Jr.

the Corinthians that the collection was not a command, but voluntary (2 Cor. 9:7).

While the New Testament does not instruct Christians to set aside a fixed percentage of income to support church leaders or church buildings, it does encourage Christians to give freely and generously to worthy causes such as aging parents, the poor, and missionaries.

The New Testament encourages giving out of abundance or prosperity. It sees giving as a blessing. It does not expect or demand sacrificial giving, though it often commends it (Luke 21:2–4, 2 Cor. 8:14, 1 Cor. 16:2, and 2 Cor. 8:8). Nevertheless, the Jewish *mitzvah* of charity and loving-kindness receives a new impetus from Christ's teaching and from the gloss upon it contained in the letters of Saint Paul. The idea that there is a specific form of love—*agape,* or "gift love," as C. S. Lewis described it in *The Four Loves*—and that this form of love is our primary religious duty becomes, in Christian thinking, the foundation of both theology and morality.

In the fourth century, the Roman Emperor Constantine converted to Christianity. Prior to Constantine's conversion, Christianity was illegal and churches met secretly in homes with part-time leaders who had other sources of income. After his conversion, Constantine made Christianity both legal and a status symbol, causing the church to expand rapidly. The church moved out of homes and into buildings and employed full-time ministers, thus creating a much greater need for income and upkeep. The tithing of the Old Law provided an obvious model and it began to be taught—more commonly in the West, however, than in the East—that the faithful should give tithes of their income. When the view began to obtain sufficient support, it found legislative expression. The Council of Macon in 585 CE ordered payment of tithes and threatened excommunication to those who refused to comply.

Catholic Christians believe in the authority of the pope, the councils, and the Bible. As such, they subscribe to the tithe as defined by the Council of Macon and later pronouncements (*Encyclicals* and *Letters*) on tithing. For Protestant Christians, relying solely on the Bible to inform their faith and practice, understanding early church practice as reflected in the New Testament resulted in some different conclusions regarding giving. For Protestants, each time the New Testament talks about tithing, it is referring to the Old Testament law requiring Jews to give 10 percent of their income to support the operation of the Temple and the Jewish priests. The Letter to the Hebrews teaches that Christ's sacrifice rendered the Temple and the priests obsolete. This is why the New Testament never applies the practice of tithing to Christians or followers of Christ.

Church reformers John Calvin and Martin Luther, both of whom saw the tithe as something to expand upon, reinforced this early understanding. They maintained that giving ought not be restricted, since all God's creation is already his and to him it must return. The ideal of being faithful and responsible stewards of all that we have is part and parcel of Reformation thought. We are trustees of what we have received, not free possessors.

The New Testament does not give exact guidance on Christian priorities when deciding whether, or how much precisely, to give to the church, missionaries, or to the poor and needy. It is worth mentioning that 1 Timothy 5:8, 1 Timothy 5:2, and Mark 7:10–13 suggest that caring for one's family and parents is the top priority of believers. The Vulgate translates *agape* as *caritas*, and the concept of charity, developed down the centuries through law and moral teaching, has a claim to be Christianity's distinctive contribution to modern ways of thinking. Exploring this concept will be one part of the story of this book.

Islam

Islam has preserved the Jewish tradition of obligatory giving, establishing as one of the five "pillars" of Islam the *zakat*, a percentage of income to be set aside for the use of the poor and to satisfy communal needs. The other four "pillars" are:

1. The declaration of faith, or *shahadah* (witness): "There is no God but the God and Muhammad is his messenger." This is a profession of faith in the oneness or unity (*tawhid*) of God.
2. Prayer. Five times a day the muezzin calls from the minaret, crying *allahu akbar*, God is most great, and Muslims must then leave off what they are doing and prostrate themselves in prayer (*salat*), which is preceded by various ritual ablutions or acts of purification. *Salat* is not a petition, but an act of worship, and a repetition of the "witness" idea, remembering God's greatness and his word. On Friday prayer is communal, in a mosque (*masjid*—place of prostration, or *jami'*, place of congregation). There is then a sermon during the midday prayers. There is no priesthood in Islam and anyone can lead the prayers—though in large mosques there tends to be a paid imam, chosen for his Qur'anic knowledge.
3. The fast of Ramadan—the ninth month of the Islamic lunar calendar. No food, drink, or sex between dawn and dusk. The fast ends with the great feast of *'Eid al-Fitr*—the feast of the breaking of the fast—which goes on Christmas-like for three days.
4. Pilgrimage (*hajj*) to Mecca, which follows Ramadan, and which each Muslim should perform at least once in his lifetime. On arriving there the pilgrim performs various rituals centered on the Ka'bah and the Plain of Arafat (place of the Prophet's last sermon), and then participates in a ritual sacrifice of animals (*'Eid al-Adha*, feast of sacrifice), commemorating the substitution of a ram for his son in Abraham's original sacrifice (though

in the Muslim view the son in question was Ismael, not Isaac).

Jihad is sometimes identified as the sixth pillar of Islam, though this has no authority in the traditions. The word means "struggle" (on behalf of the faith), and includes holy war—though no war is holy if conducted as an act of aggression rather than defense, and the duty of *jihad* is satisfied by struggling to fulfill the previous five obligations. Needless to say, this is an area of huge controversy. It has greatly affected the interpretation of *zakat* in recent years, some believing that it is legitimate to spend the money raised in this way on warlike preparations in defense of the faith—even on terrorism.

Zakat is not a ritual, but an obligation, originally to give one tenth, now 2.5 percent, of one's accumulated wealth annually, provided that wealth reaches a certain minimal level (*nisab*). In order to deal with the *zakat*, Islamic societies have established a kind of trust (*waqf*), which devotes the funds to some specific social purpose, such as education, hospitals, poor relief, or whatever. People whose hearts are to be reconciled—in other words new Muslims or those close to becoming Muslim—must follow the five pillars. Even non-Muslims are, under certain formulations, expected to be included and to pay *zakat*.

Traditional *zakat* laws generally do not cover trade. It is not permissible to pay *zakat* to some members of the family (i.e., grandparents, parents, spouses, children), for they are under the custody of the eligible man, while *zakat* is considered to be a public, not a private benefit. (This corresponds to provisions in the English common law of charity, to which I return in the next chapter.) *Zakat* doesn't become obligatory on a Muslim if he does not have a minimum amount in his possession that has remained unchanged for a whole lunar year.

According to the Shi'ite interpretation, based on the Qur'an and reported sayings of the prophet Muhammad and his household, there are two major forms of alms-giving: *khoms* ("the fifth") and *zakat*. The Shi'ites consider both types to be a personal obligation, meaning that every Muslim has the full responsibility of purifying his own money, but the governor should use no force upon any individual to give up *zakat* or *khoms*. *Khoms* ("the fifth") is taken from war loots, metals, treasures, divings (pearls), and the money that is a mix between *halal* (pure) and *haram* (taboo). *Khoms* for money involves taking the fifth of the increment or the increase in the income stored after one lunar year, and this is done after paying debts or bills (if any). *Khoms* is paid specifically for:

- Allah;
- the Messenger of Allah;
- the near relative of the Messenger (i.e., a member of the *ahl ul-bayt*);
- the orphans;
- the needy; and
- stranded travelers.

Zakat on the other hand, according to traditional Islamic teachings, is assigned to specific goods. There are nine types of goods from which *zakat* is paid out: gold, silver, camels, cows, sheep, wheat, barley, dates, and raisins. Each type has its own *nisab*, or limit under which *zakat* need not be paid.

In modern days, Muslims are more concerned with

Calouste Gulbenkian
(1869–1955)

GULBENKIAN was born in Istanbul, the son of an Armenian oil dealer. He was educated at King's College, London, in petroleum engineering. He worked in Baku, Russia, and later became a British citizen. His name is synonymous with oil. He arranged the merger of Royal Dutch/Shell. He became vastly wealthy as a result of his holdings in various oil fields and companies. His Turkish Petroleum Company had the exclusive rights to oil exploration in Iraq after World War I. He presided over the Armenian General Benevolent Union in the 1930s, which did many charitable works. During his lifetime he collected a vast art collection, which he kept at his house in Paris. Parts of it were lent to the British Museum and British National Gallery. His various holdings were held by his foundation, headquartered in Lisbon, where he died in 1955. He left some $840 million, about $300 million of which went to restore the Echmiadzin Cathedral in Armenia, which was severely damaged in World War II. The Gulbenkian Museum was established in Lisbon to display his art collection, which was left to the public.

khoms than *zakat*, mainly because few of them are farmers and own the goods by which *zakat* is paid out. On the other hand, *khoms* is given by many people, especially from the middle class and above, and is also expected from employees. It might be asked, who administers these funds, and how accountable is that person? Traditionally the funds were deposited in a *waqf* administered by the officials of the mosque. They had a religious duty to dispense them justly on recognized needs of the community. But a *waqf* is not a trust in the sense of English and American law: there is no defined class of beneficiaries, with a right to sue the trustees for malpractice. Hence more and more is the obligation to give interpreted as a private rather than a public matter, so that giving becomes a continuous thread in a Muslim's life.

Hinduism

The Hindu religion uses the term *dana* (giving) for all giving acts. *Dana* is a fertile field for understanding the meanings and justifications of giving in religious, ethical, moral, theological, political, economic, and sociological contexts. For the Hindu, giving brings name, fame, recognition, and prosperity to the giver and the family in the here and now, and enhances the quality of life after earthly death.

In Hinduism, the meritorious effects of giving persist both for the giver and for the persons in whose names the gifts are made. Through the oral traditions, venerable elders from time immemorial communicated their belief in giving. Over the course of time, written words, including epigraphic inscriptions, vividly and emphatically expressed the Hindu religion's emphasis on all acts of giving. Mutual regard and service (*Paraspara bhavana*) is one of the basic laws of life in the Hindu tradition. And giving underlies this law, which is equated with the emergence of life itself. Articulation and elaboration of this law are replete in the verbal and nonverbal expressions depicted in the Hindu religious tradition in a variety of languages and forms of symbolism.

Ethical and religious texts repeatedly talk about *dana* (giving) as an important method for purifying one's life and enhancing the quality of life here and now, everywhere and always. An attitude of sharing and giving is indeed the basic law of life in Hinduism. Why should one give, what should one give, when should one give, to whom should one give, how much should one give? Advice on these core questions has been offered in various folklore traditions, laws, and customs of Hinduism. The word *dharma* (sustainable right conduct) incorporates the act of *dana* (giving) as an important activity of human beings in personal and social behavior. *Puja* and *yajna*, terms denoting ritual and worship, also include the notion of giving to others.

In its teachings to humanity about the principles of *dharma*, the Brihadaranyaka Upanishad mentions three ingredients: be in self-control (*damyata*), be in the habit of giving (*datta*), and be compassionate (*dayadhvam*). A parable in the Upanishad describes how the thunder has been giving this Da (*damyata, datta*, and *dayadhvam*) message to humanity seasonally and forcefully: the parable is the inspiration for the section of T. S. Eliot's *The Waste Land* entitled "What the Thunder Said." The Taittiriya Upanishad says: "Give. Give with faith. Do not give without faith. Give with sensitivity. Give with a feeling of abundance. Give with right understanding."

In the "Mahabharata" epic, there are elaborate instructions on philanthropy referred to as Dana-Dharma Parva. Those instructions cover a variety of gifts such as food, water, clothing, shelter, knowledge, skills, money, silver, gold, animals, land, and manpower. Instructions also cover the appropriate occasions and justifiable qualities for the beneficiaries of such giving.

The Bhagavad Gita mentions that there are three gates open to hell for human beings: intense craving (*kama*), anger (*krodha*), and miserliness (*lobha*). By practicing worshipful attitudes (*yajna*), by acts of philanthropy (*dana*), and by insightful knowledge and right understanding (*tapah*), human beings can develop purity and feelings of right achievements. The Bhagavad Gita teachings dwell on the ethical and moral imperatives of practicing philanthropy. The meaning of giving lies in that which is given without any expectation of return and without any strings attached.

Many discussants of Hinduism have emphasized the concept of *dana*. According to Shankaracharya (eighth century CE), giving means right distribution of resources owned. Many Hindu lawgivers in their writings (*smritis*) have built philanthropic principles into life-cycle rituals and rites of passage. Every vital event of a person's life is an occasion for giving and celebration. Wrote one great Hindu social critic–poet named Sarvajna: "If oil in a lamp gets exhausted, do not flood the lamp with a barrel of oil. No barrel of oil for the lamp, but do not rest tending the lamp through spoonfuls of oil. Do not give up charity." Likewise Kabir (1398–1470), one of the great Hindu mystics and critics of formal religion and morality, challenged human beings, saying: "You came into this world with fists closed and you go away with open palms. So even while living stretch your hand open and give liberally."

In more modern times, Archarya Vinoba Bhave (1895–1982), a disciple of Mahatma Gandhi, drew on the strong philanthropic tradition of Hindu thought in developing programs of land gift (*bhudan*), village gift (*gramadan*), wealth gift (*sampattida*), and lifetime commitment (*jivan-dan*) in an effort to bring about nonviolent economic and social change through the Sarvodaya movement in India.

Buddhism

According to the Mahayana tradition of Buddhism, the essence of the eternal Buddha is compassion and concern for others, so great that it leads someone who has obtained Nirvana to turn back from the brink and help others. Such a person—the one who has attained Nirvana but turned his back on it—has in fact achieved *true* Nirvana, existence on the brink of nothingness, in which self and its concerns have entirely evaporated. Such a person is a bodhisattva, a being turned toward enlightenment, and he exists in this world as a kind of visitor from Nirvana, radiating the peace that passes understanding, which is the condition of the eternal Buddha.

The wandering mendicant has for centuries been the symbol in India of the holy way of life—a life of unattachment and renunciation, in which the body and its needs have been subdued to the overmastering spirit, and in which the world's enticements have been set aside as a dream. This image—differently embellished and with contrasting theological and institutional appendages—is common to all the great religions of India. And Buddhism is foremost in reconciling it with a viable way of life.

Indian society of Buddha's day had many holy beggars and recluses. But it did not have monastic orders. This was the great innovation that Buddha introduced: the foundation of a Buddhist community with the monastery (and later the nunnery) as its core. The term *sangha*, meaning the Buddhist community, originally referred only to the monks, and did not include the laity who, however, could benefit the monks by providing for their needs and in this way become a kind of ancillary part of the community. Since the earliest days Buddhists have affirmed their membership of the religion by reciting the "three jewels," the Buddhist equivalent of the Jewish *Shema* ("Hear Oh Israel") and the Islamic *shahadah*:

> I take refuge in the Buddha,
> I take refuge in the *Dharma*.
> I take refuge in the *Sangha*.

The term *dharma* here means the teaching of the Buddha.

The first duty of all lay-people is therefore to support the monks who set an example of renunciation that points the way to Nirvana, and makes that final state of release apparent in the midst of this world. Hence the monks are enjoined by the Buddha to respect the life of the laity:

> Remember, monks, that Brahmans and housefathers are most helpful to you, since they support you with robe and bowl, with lodging and seat, medicines and necessities in time of illness. You also, monks, are most helpful to Brahmans and housefathers, for you teach them *dharma* that is lovely at the beginning, lovely in the middle, and lovely at the end, both in spirit and in letter, and you proclaim to them the higher life in its completeness and utter purity. Thus, monks, this sublime life is lived in mutual dependence for ferrying across the flood, for the utter ending of ill. (*Itivuttakam*, 111)

Santi Deva, who lived in the seventh century CE, taught that the sacrifice of self to others is identical, in the end, to

Wafic Rida Saïd
(1939–)

 **WAFIC SAÏD** was born in Damascus, Syria, in 1939. His father, Dr. Rida Saïd, was an eye surgeon who served as minister for higher education for Syria during the late 1920s and 1930s. He also founded Syria's first university in Damascus. Wafic Saïd's current interests include music, architecture, art, and horse racing. His love of architecture and art has been demonstrated in the building of the Saïd Business School and on his family's Oxfordshire estate where Tusmore Park was awarded the prize for the "best modern house in the classical tradition."

Saïd is married to Rosemary Thompson. They have a son, Khaled, and a daughter, Rasha. He is an honorary fellow of Trinity College, Oxford, and a member of Oxford University's Court of Benefactors. Saïd started his business career in banking at UBS Geneva. He later established a project development and construction management business in Saudi Arabia. Today, Saïd is the chairman of Saïd Holdings Limited (SHL), an investment holding company with investments in Europe, North America, and the Far East.

Saïd is the benefactor and founding trustee of the Saïd Business School Foundation ($40 million donation), established to create Oxford University's business school and assist its development. Construction of the award-winning Saïd Business School was completed for the 2001–2 academic year, and it is now listed among the

(continues)

leading international business schools. The foundation now intends to assist the university in its ambitious plans to expand the work of the Saïd Business School, particularly in the field of executive education, by participating in the construction of a major additional building.

In 1982 Wafic and Rosemary Saïd founded the Karim Rida Saïd Foundation in memory of their son. The KRSF is an English charity that works to bring positive and lasting change to the lives of children and young people in the Middle East. It is nonsectarian and nonpolitical. Through its child development program, the KRSF supports the development of the most disadvantaged children in its target countries in the fields of disability, education, health, and risk reduction. Working with local partners, the foundation has funded over two hundred projects benefiting over eight thousand children. Saïd also provided substantial funding for the establishment of the laboratory at the Texas Heart Institute, St. Luke's Episcopal Hospital, in Houston, Texas.

the loss of self that leads to redemption. This, according to Santi Deva, may require an immersion in the sufferings of this world and a total devotion to those in need. In his famous poem *Bodhicaryavatara,* he writes:

> May I be a balm to the sick, their healer and servant, until sickness come never again; may I quench with rains of food and drink the anguish of hunger and thirst; may I be in the famine of the age's end their drink and meat; may I become an unfailing store for

the poor, and serve them with manifold things for their need. My own being and my pleasures, all my righteousness in the past, present and future I surrender indifferently, that all creatures may win to their end. The stillness lies in surrender of all things, and my spirit is fain for the stillness; if I must surrender all it is best to give it for fellow-creatures.

This philosophy of universal compassion goes hand in hand with an appeal to the Buddha as the source of the strength required by giving, to whom we make gifts and from whom we receive them. The Buddha himself had formulated giving—*dana*—as one element in the path of pilgrimage that the layperson could follow, so that: "Householders & the homeless [monastics] in mutual dependence both reach the true Dharma" (*Itivuttakam,* 4.7).

Generosity toward others is greatly emphasized in Mahayana as one of the perfections, as shown in Lama Tsong Khapa's *The Abbreviated Points of the Graded Path* (Tibetan: *lam-rim bsdus-don*):

Total willingness to give is the wish-granting gem
    for fulfilling the hopes of wandering beings.
It is the sharpest weapon to sever the knot of
    stinginess.
It leads to bodhisattva conduct that enhances
    self-confidence and courage,
And is the basis for universal proclamation of
    your fame and repute.
Realizing this, the wise rely, in a healthy manner,
    on the outstanding path
Of (being ever-willing) to offer completely their
    bodies, possessions, and positive potentials.

The ever-vigilant lama has practiced like that.
If you too would seek liberation,
Please cultivate yourself in the same way.

In Buddhism, giving of alms is only the beginning of one's journey to Nirvana. In practice, one can give anything with or without thought for Nirvana. This would lead to faith, the key power that one should generate within oneself for the Buddha, *dharma* and *sangha*: for the supreme example, his teachings and his community.

According to the ancient Pali canon: "Of all gifts [alms], the gift of dharma (dhamma) is the highest."

Native American and Aboriginal

According to the "gift economy," as practiced by most Native American tribes as well as by many aboriginal peoples from other parts of the world, status is given to individuals based on what people give to others rather than on what they have collected or produced.

"Potlatch" is a Chinook adaptation of the Nootka word *patshatl*, which means "giving." A Native American potlatch celebrates the giving and distribution of a portion of wealth among fellow tribe members. These ceremonies also serve to mark transfers of power between generations, to memorialize important chieftains, and to celebrate the social initiations of heirs.

Cultures that have an unstable system of currency or for which there is no monetary system or agreed exchange, practice barter, that is, the exchange of goods and services for other goods and services. Barter giving was practiced by all of the Native American tribal cultures and also by aboriginals in Australia and the Pacific Islands. And many

Native Americans and aboriginals viewed institutionalized giving (exemplified by barter and potlatch) as a way to honor future generations and clan members. Both barter and potlatch demonstrate the Native American philosophy that giving should be mutual and equal among all parties.

Historically, the definitions of giving and values of wealth were so different between Native American and European American culture that there was a gap in understanding and often a barrier of exchange and trust between the cultures. Until European Americans became the dominant culture in North America, Native Americans existed as hunters and gatherers, surviving by taking only what they needed from the world and the land and interacting with one another in a gift economy that relied on an understanding of trade, barter, and wealth distribution.

Confucianism

Confucian philosophy, prevalent in China and other parts of Asia, holds that there is a basic order in the universe and a natural harmony linking man, nature, and the cosmos (heaven). It also holds that man is by nature a social being, and that the natural order of the universe should be reflected in human relations. The family unit is seen as the primary social unit; relationships within the family were fundamental to all others and comprised three of the "five relationships" that were the model for all others: sovereign-subject; husband-wife; parent-child; elder brother–younger brother; friend-friend.

In this hierarchy of social relations, each role had clearly defined duties; reciprocity or mutual responsibility between subordinate and superior was fundamental to the

Confucian concept of human relations. The virtue of filial piety, or devotion of the child to his parents, was the foundation for all others. When extended to all human beings, it nurtured the highest virtue, humaneness (*rén* or *jen*), or the sense of relatedness to other persons.

In traditional China it was assumed by adherents of all Confucian schools of thought that government would be monarchical and that the state had its model in the family. The ruler was understood to be at once the son of heaven, and the father of the people, ruling under the Mandate of Heaven. Traditional thinkers, reflecting on the problem of government, were concerned primarily not with changing institutions and laws but with ensuring the moral uprightness of the ruler and encouraging his appropriate conduct as a father figure. The magistrate, the chief official of the lowest level of government and the official closest to the people, was known as the "father-mother" official. Even today, under a radically different form of government, the Chinese term for state is *guo-jia*, or "nation-family," suggesting the survival of the idea of this paternal and consensual relationship. The first and third of the "five relationships"—i.e., emperor and minister, father and son—indicate the parallels between family and state.

The notion of the role of the state as guarantor of the people's welfare developed very early, along with the monarchy and the bureaucratic state. It was also assumed that good government could bring about order, peace, and the good society. Government was the agency for charity, not the individual. Tests of the good ruler were social stability, population growth (a reflection of ancient statecraft where the good ruler was one who could attract people from other states), and ability to create conditions that fostered the people's welfare. The Mandate of Heaven was understood as justifying the right to rule, with the corollary right to rebel against a ruler who did not fulfill his duties to the people. The state played a major role in determining water rights, famine control and relief, and ensuring social stability. The state encouraged people to grow rice and other grains rather than commercial crops in order to ensure an adequate food supply; it held reserves in state granaries, in part to lessen the effects of drought and floods, particularly common in northern China. For fear of losing the Mandate of Heaven, governments levied very low taxes, which often meant that the government could not provide all the services expected of it, and that officials ended up extorting money from the people.

In Confucian tradition, *li*, though still linked to traditional forms of action, came to point toward the balance between maintaining these norms so as to perpetuate an ethical social fabric, and violating them in order to accomplish ethical good. These concepts are about doing the proper thing at the proper time, and are connected to the belief that training in the *li* that past sages have devised cultivates in people virtues that include ethical judgment about when *li* must be adapted in light of situational contexts.

In early Confucianism, *yi* and *li* are closely linked terms. *Yi* can be translated as righteousness, though it may simply mean what is ethically best to do in a certain context. The term can be contrasted with action done out of self-interest. While pursuing one's own self-interest is not necessarily bad, one would be a better, more righteous person if one based one's life upon following a path designed to enhance the greater good, an outcome of *yi*. This is doing the right thing for the right reason. *Yì* is also based upon reciprocity.

Just as action according to *lì* should be adapted to conform to the aspiration of adhering to *yì*, so *yì* is linked to the core value of *rén*. *Rén* is the virtue of perfectly fulfilling one's responsibilities toward others, most often translated as "benevolence" or "humaneness"; translators have also called it "goodness" and "selflessness." Confucius' moral system was based upon empathy and understanding others, rather than divinely ordained rules. To develop one's spontaneous responses of *rén* so that these could guide action intuitively was even better than living by the rules of *yì*.

To promote the attentiveness to *rén*, Confucius articulated what can be seen as an early version of the Golden Rule: "What one does not wish for oneself, one ought not to do to anyone else; what one recognizes as desirable for oneself, one ought to be willing to grant to others."

Modern Secular Philosophy

The rise of secular society during the Enlightenment went hand in hand with the development of moral theories that tried to derive human rights and duties from purely secular premises, without reference either to natural law or the revealed will of God. Whether or not these theories have succeeded in providing a foundation for ordinary morality, it is noteworthy that they have all made room for gift and generosity as a fundamental part of the moral order. Thus for Hume and Adam Smith, morality is founded on sympathy and benevolence—the concern for others that leads us to consider their needs and sufferings as on a par with our own.

Li Ka-shing
(1928–)

LI KA-SHING is one of the wealthiest businesspersons in the world and likely the richest of Chinese descent. His wealth is estimated at over $26 billion. He is chairman of Hutchison Whampoa and Cheung Kong Holdings, based in Hong Kong. His companies are the largest operator of container terminals and the largest health and beauty retailers globally.

Known for his thrifty lifestyle, Li Ka-shing has become Asia's most generous philanthropist. He is said to have donated over $1 billion to charitable causes to date. Born in Guangdong Province, China, he fled to Hong Kong in 1940. Leaving school at age fifteen, Li labored long days and eventually started his own real estate company, then acquired others and branched out to other industries.

His life has been called a "lesson in integrity and adaptability." Remaining true to his internal compass, he has been able to build a business empire. It covers every facet of life from electricity to telecoms, from real estate to retail, and from shipping to the Internet. Li Ka-shing has been honored with many awards and honors, including the Order of the British Empire.

Pledging a third of his wealth to charity has led Li to found a university near his hometown near Chaozhou, China, with a Buddhist orientation. He has donated libraries, faculties of medicine, and hospitals and has given generously to various aid and relief efforts,

(continues)

earthquake disasters, and recently to Singapore's Lee Kuan Yew School of Public Policy at the National University of Singapore.

For Rousseau, society is or ought to be founded on a social contract according to which each person counts for one and the interests and desires of all are consulted—a society in which selfishness is extinguished in the General Will. For Kant, the root of morality is the "categorical imperative," which instructs us to act only on that maxim that we can will as a law for all mankind (Kant's version of the Golden Rule), and also to treat people (self and other) as ends in themselves and never as instruments through which to pursue selfish interests.

The tendency of all these secular philosophies is toward the very conclusion that, as we have seen, has been advanced by the great world religions and the traditions that have sprung from them. No less than religious moral thinking, secular morality tells us to live for others, not merely for ourselves. Secularism is a humanitarian philosophy that promotes equality, rights, and duties. Philanthropy as a rather generalized moral project is not sufficient, it is argued, unless it is rooted in a considered political philosophy and connected to some wider political and economic framework of rights and duties. The Enlightenment relied to a large extent on natural law principles (e.g., as in Providence and Nature's God). Giving, according to various modern secular interpretations, is of course entirely optional, self-determined, and is neither mandated from on high or by the state.

Concluding Thoughts

And so we can see that in virtually every tradition (religious as well as secular) humankind has known—every faith community on every continent and also among those who are agnostic or even atheistic—there exists a diverse set of teachings that emphasize generosity. Being generous is, I would therefore argue, not just a core part of the human condition, but a universal moral urge, our defining nature. Since generosity so defines our human nature, it is one of the few things on which people around the entire globe, though on different pathways, can agree.

There is a long religious history of wisdom, commonly defined as the judicious application of knowledge. The *Book of Wisdom* is part of the Roman Catholic Bible. Nearly every religious tradition venerates wise thinking and the persons who do it. The Jewish proverb "fear of God is the beginning of all wisdom" (Prov. 1:7) is not atypical. For the ancient Hebrews, this fear started with hating evil, arrogance, and pride. The wisdom of giving, and of giving generously as a habit, can also be traced to premodern times. In fact, generosity as a virtue has long been considered a central part of wisdom.

Seeds of unity have been planted around the world throughout the ages. I believe it is not too much to hope that today, in a world beset by momentous choices and unprecedented problems, people will take a closer look at the virtue of generosity and, as a result of this examination, seek and work toward a global community and local communities united by giving.

Remember, however, that giving is not exclusively for the rich. The widow gave her "mite," and it was more generous than the rich young ruler. Giving is for everyone.

Charity and Gift 2

Though I speak with the tongues of men and of angels, but have not charity, I am only a resounding gong or a clanging cymbal. If I give all I possess to the poor and surrender my body to the flames, but have not charity, I gain nothing.

ST. PAUL, I COR. 13:1, 3

WE HAVE SEEN that the major religions all understand "gift" as fundamental to living rightly in God's eyes and in the eyes of our fellow human beings. In this brief chapter, I will dig a bit more deeply into my own tradition of Christian thinking, rooted in the New Testament, and particularly in the wonderful insights of St. Paul.

This tradition is actually of great relevance to all serious people, not least because it is an attempt to spell out in detailed terms exactly what it means to live in the belief that the world is ordered—ordered by a loving God, who demands love from each of us, not toward himself only but toward our neighbors. Who are our neighbors, next door and around the globe? As the parable of the Good Samaritan makes clear, neighbors include those whom we come across but with whom we have no other connection, not even one of tribe, nation, or faith (Luke 10:25–37). It is the Christian tradition that has shaped our Western culture and its understanding of the concept of charity as "the love to which we are commanded," to use Kant's striking words.

Christianity is rooted in the conviction that the world is ordered by a loving God, who demands love from each of us, love directed not only toward himself but toward our neighbors. The concept of giving lies at the very heart of Christian theology. Galatians 1:4 states that Jesus Christ "gave himself for our sins, that he might deliver us from this present evil world." Galatians 2:20 affirms that Christ "loved me" and as a result "gave himself for me." No wonder Paul expressed his gratitude with these words, "Thanks be unto God for his unspeakable gift" (2 Cor. 9:15). Over and over again in the New Testament (see Matt. 20:28, 1 Tim. 2:6, Titus 2:14), we are told how Christ gave his very life for our sakes. Sacrificial giving is central to everything that is identified with Christian living.

Then there is the giving of ourselves. St. Paul in 2 Corinthians 8:5 tells of the Macedonians, who did more than just give for the needs of others, "but first gave their own selves to the Lord, and unto us by the will of God." True Christian giving begins with the giving of ourselves to the Lord. Paul beseeched the Romans to "present your bodies a living sacrifice, holy, acceptable unto God, which is your reasonable service" (Rom 12:1). More than anything else, God wants you. And anything you give without giving yourself is only a token of what is owed to the Lord.

Christians also are instructed to give to the saints. Romans 12:13 suggests that believers should be "distributing to the necessity of the saints; given to hospitality." Those Christians who have this world's goods should be "rich in good works, ready to distribute, willing to communicate" (1 Tim. 6:18). Notice that these commands are not to the church but to individuals. In fact, the Bible's command to help those in need is always given to individual believers. This is not to say that churches are to refrain from helping the poor, only that the bulk of the responsibility goes to the individual.

More directly to the theme of this book, Christians are particularly and repeatedly instructed to give to the poor. James teaches (James 2:15–16) that immediate action is required when fellow Christians are lacking in either of two areas: if (1) they are naked (without adequate covering) or if (2) they need daily food. When they see this kind of desperate need in a brother or sister in Christ, they are to give them "those things which are needful to the body."

The Bible instructs followers to love their neighbors. And in his parable of the Good Samaritan, Jesus makes it clear that our neighbors are not just the people who live next door. Our neighbors include those with whom we have no immediate or obvious connection. Our neighbors are people from other ethnic groups, other nations, and other religious faiths. Some are closer in proximity to us than others, thus we know them better. But even those who live at a distance can be neighbors. The growing interconnectedness of people around the globe has enabled us more and more to appreciate this reality. The bottom line is that, for the Christian, a neighbor is someone whom we encounter and whose need we observe and to which we have the opportunity to respond by giving, providing whatever it is our neighbor needs.

Jesus condensed the Law of the Prophets into two great commandments: "You shall love the Lord your God with

The Maclellan Family

OF SCOTTISH ANCESTRY, the family started Provident Life & Accident Insurance Company in the 1880s in Tennessee. They opened a family foundation in 1945 and have been very active since in spiritual, educational, and civic causes, especially in their home location, Chattanooga. Their primary giving more recently has been to missions around the world. As a multigenerational trust, the family's faith in God fuels all their charitable giving. The attempt is made to apply lessons learned in business to philanthropy. With over $300 million in assets, they have become a major giver to nearly every evangelical cause. The mission statement is "to extend the Kingdom of God in accordance with the Great Commission." Members of the family give a minimum of 70 percent of their yearly income to charity.

your whole heart, with your whole soul, and with your whole mind. . . . You shall love your neighbor as yourself" (Matt. 22:37–39). I was taught in Sunday school to visualize this as a cross. Vertically, God and man find each other; and, horizontally, man finds and helps his fellows. They are completely intertwined. He might well have whispered, "Be a good steward" in reply to the question, "Lord, what must I do to be saved?"

The Apostle Paul emphasizes a distinctive brand of love. In his first letter to the Corinthians, he delivers his celebrated encomium of the three theological virtues: faith, hope, and charity. The word he uses for charity—*agape*—denotes a new kind of love, a love that has been brought to the world by Christ, a love that God extends to all and that all of us are asked to extend to one another. This "gift love" is not, as St. Paul makes clear, a form of bargaining or negotiation. It does not lay down terms or aim for some selfish advantage. Unlike the *eros* of the Greeks, it is not an interested passion, nor does it claim exclusive rights. It is an entirely disinterested form of love. It is caring for the other as a person, and relating to him or her on equal terms. It is also free of charge, which makes it distinct among our usual loves and likings.

From St. Paul's discussion we inherit the concept of "charity" as a specific form of giving, particularly giving to those in need. As I will discuss more fully in chapter 3, we give to others as an expression of gratitude for what we have and in recognition that the world is ordered by the principle of gift. *Being* itself, St. Thomas Aquinas argued, is the fundamental gift, granted by God to himself by his own nature and to the world by God's choice. Thus, according to Christian theology, life itself is a gift, as are all the good things that have come to me and to you, good things that come from the source that granted life.

Once we see the world in this way, which is the way of faith, we can see the reality of gift love and can begin to understand how the world is ordered by its power. The chains of gift and gratitude spread through all things, and our spiritual well-being depends on linking to them. They are not heavy chains or burdensome. To the contrary, their main ingredient is freedom. As we will see later, by linking to these chains we receive a benefit far greater than the ones we bestow.

Stewardship Spirituality 3

*Grace is but glory begun, and glory
is but grace perfected.*

JONATHAN EDWARDS

IN 1674, an Anglican priest named Thomas Ken wrote a hymn titled "Awake My Soul and with the Sun." He wrote this hymn for choirboys at Winchester College to use in their private devotions. The final stanza contained the words, "Praise God, from Whom all blessings flow / Praise Him, all creatures here below / Praise Him above, ye heavenly host / Praise Father, Son, and Holy Ghost."

Over time, this last stanza came into widespread use as the Doxology (from the Greek *doxa*, "glory," and *logos,* "word"). Commonly sung at offering time across many Christian denominations, the Doxology is arguably the most often sung piece of music in all of worship.

A spirituality of stewardship begins with a thorough understanding of the concept of grace. Understanding grace, in turn, begins with an affirmation that, as the Doxology proclaims, all blessings flow from God.

Grace is commonly defined as the sovereign favor of God for humankind—especially with regard to salvation—

irrespective of actions, earned worth, or proven goodness. The very fact that people are allowed to live, that they are sustained, that they thrive, stems from the grace of God. You can't buy grace—it is not for sale. God's grace is, rather, a free gift, which makes it seem almost too good to be true. In fact it is.

Most everyone has heard the words and music to the hymn "Amazing Grace." This hymn is sung at funerals, baseball games, you name it. Both words and music are memorable, even gripping, especially when accompanied with bagpipes. The powerful story behind the words is that of their author, John Newton, who was converted from swashbuckling slave trader to saintly priest. It has been often told in books and movies. And it is a compelling story precisely because it presents us with the image of "grace abounding to the chief of sinners," as John Bunyan had put it a century before Newton's ministry. The words "grace of God" are music in a believer's ears, and have a salvific power of their own. The words are often repeated in the rosary. They famously feature in Dr. Johnson's humble remark, pointing to a beggar in the streets of London: "There, but for the Grace of God, go I." They are music because they signal salvation. They sum up the very essence of the religious life: the life of faith, hope, and charity.

The word "grace" (Latin, *gratia*) itself means a supernatural gift of God. In Christianity, theologically, Jesus Christ, as a child, was endowed with God's grace. "And the child grew and became strong; he was filled with wisdom, and the grace of God was upon him" (Luke 2:40, NIV). Jesus entered his earthly ministry filled with God's grace. "The Word became flesh and made his dwelling among us. We have seen his glory, the glory of the One and Only, who came from the Father, full of grace and truth" (John 1:14,

NIV). God's grace flowed through Christ to all of us. "For the law was given through Moses; grace and truth came through Jesus Christ" (John 1:17, NIV).

The entire human race benefits from God's grace. It is obvious that his divine grace is extended to believers, but it is extended to unbelievers too: "Though grace is shown to the wicked, they do not learn righteousness; even in a land of uprightness they go on doing evil and regard not the majesty of the Lord" (Isa. 26:10, NIV). This common grace allows people to be born, grow up, live their lives, and make a choice.

Perhaps we can come to a greater appreciation of grace by considering some of ways the term "grace" has come to be used. For example, we speak of someone giving way "with good grace." We speak of a graceful act or of someone who displays a gracious manner. In all such idioms we are referring to the way in which human giving spontaneously appeals to us, endears us to the giver, and makes him or her stand forth in some way from the ordinary utilitarian transactions of human life.

Grace, in this sense, reminds us of the nobility of giving, and especially when what is given is not a material thing, but something perhaps far more difficult to relinquish, such as time, pride, and self-opinion. Losing with good grace is widely regarded as a great moral accomplishment. We teach it to our children with the same emphasis we place on kindness and consideration. The one who loses with good grace is the one who can truly give himself in the moment when it is hardest to do so, when he risks loss of face, loss of standing, loss of self-esteem.

From this moral sense of "grace," it is a small step to the aesthetic sense. The grace of the gazelle, the graceful lines of a dress, the graceful melodies of Mozart—all such things are visions of a higher purpose in the scheme of things, in which harmony, peace, and order prevail. We teach our children not merely to behave with "good grace," but to make graceful gestures and to use graceful language. It seems that grace has so thoroughly penetrated our world that we find it in virtually every area of human interest and human experience.

It is not surprising to find that grace in all its senses was condensed by the artists and poets of the Middle Ages into a single image: the image of the Virgin Mary, the graceful woman, who received the gift of grace with a very human grace of her own and who became the ideal of feminine beauty, unforgettably portrayed for us by Lippi, Bellini, and Fra Angelico. The great prayer with which she is still addressed begins with the words with which she herself was once addressed, by the angel of the Lord: "Hail Mary, full of grace . . ."

My faith, too, was dependent on a sense of a transcendent grace. As a young person who grew up singing hymns, I still recall with fondness the melodies and words of old favorites that touched the soul and swayed the congregation of the faithful. I find it regrettable that few hymns are written today. I consider it a sign that our spiritual capital is not renewing itself as energetically as it could. But it may also be because those old hymns are so complete, so satisfying, and so little in need of replacement.

I recall in particular an old, early nineteenth-century hymn that was sung in my Philadelphia Presbyterian church. It was written by John Gurney, who was likely recalling his own beautiful western Scottish island of Arran, off the Firth of Clyde. "Fair Waved the Golden Corn" reminds us of whose world this is and of the generosity we are called to in it. Here are its moving lyrics:

Fair waved the golden corn, In Canaan's pleasant land,
When full of joy, some shining morn, Went forth the
reaper band.

To God so good and great, Their cheerful thanks they
pour; Then carry to His temple gate, The choicest of
their store.

Like Israel, Lord, we give, Our earliest fruits to Thee,
And pray that, long as we shall live, We may Thy
children be.

Thine is our youthful prime, And life and all its pow-
ers, Be with us in our morning time, And bless our
evening hours.

In wisdom let us grow, As years and strength are given,
That we may serve Thy Church below, And join Thy
saints in Heaven.[1]

Grace is an enabling power sufficient for humankind's
redemption and spiritual progress. Grace divine, while a
free gift, is also an indispensable gift from God. Without
it there are certain and real limitations, weaknesses, flaws,
impurities, and faults (such as carnality) that humankind simply cannot overcome. Therefore, it is necessary
to increase in God's grace if we are to complete and perfect ourselves. This increase involves a lifetime of spiritual
work and discipline. Perfection is always something we
strive toward—a journey never quite completed. Yet we can
know when we are making some progress down the road.

Responding to Grace

Those who understand grace are able to affirm that life
itself is God's gift and that everything, *every thing* in this
world, comes from him. An understanding of grace is the

Sebastian Spering Kresge
(1867–1966)

KRESGE FOUNDED the S. S. Kresge Company, the nation's first chain of five-and-ten-cent stores, in Detroit, Michigan, in 1899. By 1912 when the company was incorporated, American families were shopping at eighty-five Kresge retail locations. The son of a hard-working Pennsylvania farmer, Sebastian made an initial $1.6 million gift to establish The Kresge Foundation in 1924 for the "promotion of human progress." Today, eight decades later, the foundation has an endowment of nearly $3.1 billion and is guided by a board of trustees that includes Kresge family members; all share Sebastian's philanthropic desire to improve the quality of life for future generations. The foundation supports nonprofit organizations working in six fields of interest: health, the environment, community development, arts and culture, education, and human services.

key that unlocks the door to the true meaning of generosity and also to a genuine experience of joy and happiness.

Those who truly understand the meaning of grace ultimately have just one way to respond, and that is with gratitude. Indeed, the natural response to gift is gratitude. The grace of God is the beginning of all generosity and the origin of both gift and gratitude.

For those who understand this, giving is not a mere duty. Rather, it becomes a foremost pleasure. It is a way of opening up yourself to another, of putting yourself at another person's service. It is an invitation to friendship.

There is a strong correlation between societies in which gift is prominent and societies in which gratitude unites people to their benefactors. But gratitude goes beyond people thanking those who have helped them. There is a natural tendency for the grateful person to want to "give back" to others. We see this vividly across America, where people will give to the schools and colleges that have educated them and to the hospitals that have cared for them. Many give their time, knowledge, and energy by volunteering, a characteristic that stood out to Alexis de Tocqueville in his journeys through the American hinterland nearly two centuries ago.[2] And it is a feature of which we are rightly proud, for in many ways this giving culture defines America and Americans at their very best.

This is not as common in Europe, where by and large the state has taken charge of those who have been deemed to need help. When someone receives something as a "right" rather than a gift, then gratitude is not just inappropriate, it is quite impossible, for any expression of gratitude would signify that person did not believe that he or she had a right to what was received. The system assumes otherwise, thus, "If what you are giving me is my right, then it is something you owe me; to be grateful would be to deny my ownership."

On the whole, socialism in any form has shown itself to be hostile to private giving. Such giving does not merely marginalize the state, but also demonstrates too much respect for private property, industry, and wealth—commodities that are hardly compatible with the socialist objective of a strictly equal society in which nobody has more than anybody else.

We should not be surprised, therefore, that one of the first acts of Lenin after the Bolshevik Revolution in Russia was to abolish and expropriate all private charities. The same happened in other countries that fell under the Soviet yoke after World War II. When the communists took over Hungary, there were some ten thousand voluntary societies in that tiny country of eight million souls. Every one was abolished within two years. Charity was made illegal—as in all other communist countries. Gift, as the sign and symbol of private property, and of a life in freedom outside the control of the state, was anathema to the Communist Party, as it is in China today. People had to give in secret and at risk of imprisonment. Underground schools and universities, underground churches, and underhand medicine survived—but only thanks to heroic actions by the few, and without any recognition, needless to say, from the fellow-traveling governments in Western Europe, many of which shared the socialist assumption that it is for the state after all, not the individual, to provide to those in need.

These societies were and are being deprived both of the joy of giving and the joy of expressing gratitude. They dismiss the argument of this book that giving is not only natural, but is also a fundamental ingredient of moral health. By giving we recognize the existence of the other as a free being fulfilled through love. And by feeling gratitude we acknowledge our own freedom, our dependency on others, and our need to love and be loved. Remove gift and gratitude from human society, and what remains is not a community but a "lonely crowd," in the famous words of the sociologist David Riesman.[3]

This analysis is by no means meant to suggest that freer, capitalist societies have automatically led to healthy views of stewardship, though certainly they offer a greater potential for such. The truth is that, regardless of the prevailing economic system, stewardship makes no sense in a culture of "me" where winning is defined by what people take and status determined by what they own.

On the Thanksgiving holiday, some families go around the table with each member saying for what they are most thankful. Some find this traditional exercise embarrassing or corny. The reason it is so difficult or awkward nowadays is because we have gotten out of the habit of having a thankful attitude. Rather, we have increasingly come to expect, even demand things. We want the turkey and the dressings, but none of spirit that they symbolize. Some have come to disrespect saying "thank you" and to dislike the very act of giving.

Thus for many, a healthy spirituality of stewardship will require a change of heart. In fact, it turns out that the heart is a much more powerful organ than your cardiologist or your latest electrocardiograph ever told you. We often use a concrete object to express an abstract idea. Most people associate the heart with more than a body organ that pumps and circulates blood, although that is what it is and what it does. It has long been associated with human emotions such as love, even kindness in phrases like, "He or she has a good heart," or its opposite, "He or she is heartless."

The ancient Hebrews saw the heart as the seat of all emotions and the senses. Unlike us, they also saw it as the center of all thought. The heart for them had the many functions that we now attribute to the brain. The ancient Hebrews believed the heart was the mind and as such, the core of our being, the center of all thought and emotion. When in ancient Israel they were told "to love God with all their hearts" (Deut. 6:5), it was not merely an emotional attachment, something romantic or sentimental, but rather meant to keep all thoughts on him. The very symbols used in the ancient Hebrew language to depict the word heart—*lev*, לֵב—are first, the shepherd staff representing authority, as a shepherd has over his flock; and second, a picture of a floor with a tent, representing the idea of being inside it, as a family would reside in a tent. When combined, they mean "the authority within." The heart is the powerful center of being.

Thus, a healthy spirituality of stewardship can be shaped not only by what we feel in our hearts, but by what we do, by the choices we make with our minds. Whether a person is financially "comfortable" or has only modest means, the choices that person makes about what to do with the gifts he or she has received—gifts of talent, energy, influence, time, and resources—provide a remarkably accurate picture of the shape of his or her soul. Those who hoard their gifts, living with clenched fists, suffer the sadness of a pinched soul and a miserly existence. They never experience the extravagant blessings that come to those who live with open hands and giving hearts.

Once again, if a transformation is to take place and if stewardship is to become a way of life—a kind of "life-principle" that touches every corner of life—it must begin with gratitude, with genuine thanksgiving to God for all his wonderful gifts to us. The United States Conference of Catholic Bishops' *Stewardship: A Disciple's Approach* expressed the idea that the practice of stewardship has the power to change both our self-understanding and our contextual understanding of the meaning of our lives. To paraphrase the letter, "steward-disciples recognize God as the origin of life, the giver of freedom, the source of all they have and are. They see themselves as caretakers of God's gifts.[4]

If our treasures are manifold and if they emanate from God, then giving them back to him and sharing them with others makes infinite sense. It sounds wise and, perhaps, self-apparent. In fact, it only makes "infinite" sense. It makes no sense whatsoever if the time scale is any shorter than eternity. If the time horizon were any shorter, the impulse would in all actuality be to hoard the treasures or to keep them for yourself and not to deploy them at all.

I once entered the gothic St. Nicholas Cathedral in Fribourg, Switzerland, on the German-French-speaking border. In traversing the seven-hundred-year-old splendid antique structure, I happened across a modern-looking brochure amongst all the historical accounts in the rack. Since its title was "Abundance Through Stewardship," it interested me greatly, so I picked it up. On the outside was a silhouette of a man with his arms outstretched and a single Bible verse: John 16:24—"Ask, and you will receive. That your joy may be full." I opened it up and it had a valuable message around three themes, God's abundance, trust, and stewardship. The argument was different from most Catholic or Protestant tracts I have seen. It stated:

> "Stewardship" is about God's abundance and our trust in that abundance. God never runs out because he is fullness itself; always there for the asking. The difficulty with abundance lies in our inability to trust. How do we build up trust? By praying, "I believe, help my unbelief." Trust is only the beginning. Giving back to God a measure of what He gives reflects

George Cadbury
(1839–1922)

Born in Birmingham, West Midlands, England, Cadbury had a knack for making money. He was also dedicated to God's kingdom. As a member of the Society of Friends (Quakers), he believed wealth was entrusted to help others. His family candy business was profitable. He gave away profits and supported missions at home and abroad. Cadbury was keenly interested in innovative social reforms and industrial relations. His motto was "humble before God." With his brother Richard, he expanded his father's cocoa and chocolate business. They established workers' villages that were a prototype for modern housing and town planning. He agitated for political action on national old age pensions and insurance. Besides giving very generously to charities, he sought the elimination of harsh labor conditions.

another aspect of God's laws—the more you give, the more God will give to you.

The brochure went on to stress that this is true in every area of life. In this sense then, stewardship should actually be seen as an *opportunity* to share your gifts with both God and creation. The piece ended with some striking language from the *Book of Common Prayer*. It said that in the end stewardship comes down to one very simple concept: "Go in peace, to love and serve the Lord." While this was a message from a European Catholic Church, it is, I think, indicative of the emerging and transcultural view of stewardship that appears to be arising in many places, from Africa to America, and from Asia across Europe. It's a growing understanding that generosity ultimately isn't about money but rather is rooted in an attitude of the heart.

Any true and full definition of stewardship must include prayer and sacrifice, for without these the self, and not the other, will still occupy the center of our thinking. Stewardship is not some Faustian bargain or a form of long-term hedonism directed to the happy afterlife. It is nothing more than a "living" faith, here and now, next door, across the nation and around the globe. Consider that even stewarding the earth—caring for the land, what has been called "earthkeeping"—is a form of giving that is increasingly understood and practiced as an obligation to God, our ancestors, and to future generations, an obligation to conserve and protect what has been entrusted to us.

In sum, healthy stewardship spirituality begins with an understanding of grace; continues with a response of gratitude; includes commitments to prayer, meditation, and sacrifice; and ends with a life full of contentment and joy.

Time, Treasure, and Talent 4

> *We make a living by what we get, but we make a life by what we give.*
>
> SIR WINSTON CHURCHILL

PEOPLE WHO ATTEND church regularly sometimes get less than positive feelings upon noticing in the bulletin that the sermon has something to do with stewardship. Many instinctively want to head for the door because they think the offering plate is going to get passed around and they are going to be asked to make a pledge, perhaps for a year or more. However, true stewardship is not just "paying up," writing a check once every now and again and then being done with it. Giving money and nothing else constitutes a rather cheap response to grace, for, truthfully, stewardship is so much more. In fact, stewardship, properly understood, is a way of life. It consists of continually receiving God's gifts gratefully and constantly sharing God's gifts abundantly. And it has to do with much more than money, important as that is.

Jesus says in Luke 12:34, "For where your treasure is, there will your heart be also." Does his use of the word "treasure" here mean "money"? Is our only treasure the pot of gold some pirates buried in their booty on a beach in the Caribbean Sea? Of course not. Humans are endowed with many treasures, many gifts, one of which is surely the wealth they have worked for, saved, and invested over time. But that is only one of dozens of kinds of treasure. Treasure comes in every shape, color, size, and form. Literally, it is whatever is of value—*capital*—human, social, financial, intellectual—every kind of asset ever discovered or invented.

In Judaism, one does not even have to have money to be a giver. The classic ethical work *Paths of the Righteous* enumerates three main categories of generosity: giving of one's wealth, giving of oneself physically, and giving of one's wisdom.[1] Each is seen as the equal of the other.

Charity—the disinterested love of others—can be shown in many ways and forms. The schoolteacher who stays behind after class to help her slower pupils gives to them something more precious than wealth, and that is time, encouragement, and concern. The businessman who forgoes the opportunity to increase his own wealth in order to run a youth club or coach a team in a deprived neighborhood gives something that no gift of money could supply, which is the confidence and self-esteem that enable his pupils to give and receive in turn and so to enter the greater society from which they might otherwise feel excluded.

The stewardship of time is every bit as important, maybe even more important, than the stewardship of wealth. In our crazy world of busy schedules, it is a virtue that needs to be constantly before our minds. Most senior executives I know admit that time is their most precious commodity. But you cannot manufacture any more of it, borrow it at a bank, or buy it retail.

William Wilberforce
(1759–1833)

THE SON of a wealthy English merchant from Hull, Wilberforce has become synonymous with abolition. His life was recently made famous in the full-length movie *Amazing Grace*. His father died when he was a boy, and his aunt and uncle, who were supporters of John Wesley and the Methodist movement, brought him up. He attended St. John's College, Oxford, where he was stunned by the drunken and lewd behavior. His best friend became William Pitt, who went on to become the youngest prime minister of Britain. Wilberforce himself went into politics at age twenty, as a Tory, running against the wealthy Lord Rockingham. In 1784 he converted to the evangelical cause and joined the Clapham Sect, which was interested in social reform and an end to the slave trade. With the Quakers he took up abolition with a real zeal. His first bills in Parliament were roundly defeated, but eventually were enacted (in 1807) in both Houses. The former slave trader turned Anglican priest, John Newton, had a profound impact on Wilberforce. Always a philanthropist, Wilberforce worked vigorously for public charities, giving both his own considerable wealth and time. His pursuits in giving were aimed at good manners and institutions to educate the poor and women.

Consider that each person born in America now has approximately 73 years to live, or about 38,368,800 minutes in their normal life expectancy. Men have a little less and women a little more. Life on earth is, in a word, *finite*. It is running out from the minute the clock begins to tick. It is true that we are as a species living longer. But no one lives forever. Even the Romanians in those happy Dannon yogurt commercials live only to be 106 or so. They too expire. The sooner we come to see the reality of limited physical life, of our own humanity and finiteness, the better off we are. We are humbled. We realize that we are terminal beings in our nature and longevity.

In opposition to this realization, people either indulge in fantasies of eternity on earth, or they give up on life as something accidental and meaningless. The conception of life as a proud self-assertion, which eternally recurs so that we become gods by willing ourselves to be so, is one that Nietzsche put before us. But it is a conception that ought not to distract us from the total failure of his own attempt to be other than a timid and intimidated weakling. The opposite view of life, as a meaningless struggle, which Camus put before us in *The Myth of Sisyphus*, simply leaves us with one decision to make—when to commit suicide.

Neither of those visions has any relevance to someone who sees life as it is. Riches and fame do not confer immortality: in all truth after a few generations your relatives and descendants will know neither your name nor your significance. As for the meaning of life, it is not to be found in any achievement or transformation. It lies in accepting our being here on earth, bound by the passage of time, inexorably moving on the path that ends in death. The name for that acceptance is gratitude. We accept our temporal nature by giving, for by giving we receive—receive our own mortal existence as the most precious of gifts, as the opportunity to become what we should be.

The truly realistic question, therefore, is how we choose to live the amount of time that is allotted to us. Recall Tolkien's famous line (spoken by Gandalf) from *The Lord of the Rings*: "All we have to decide is what to do with the time that is given us."[2] Do we give that time to others for shared purposes, or do we hoard it selfishly? Do we spend our lives in order to gain them in the classical definition? Do we in the process honor God and express our gratitude? Time is short even in a world where time is redefined as speed. Overnight, next day, just in time, right now, instant this, faster that. However you see it, time is a defined span that is entrusted to us to use responsibly, and that means to use it in a spirit of service. Service to whom? One answer is service to others and service to God. Bob Dylan produced a whole album with the nagging question, "Who do you serve?" He knew "you gotta serve somebody."

There is a theory of stewardship that became very popular a decade or so ago. It is well intentioned but wrong. It is called "half time." It works like this. You work as hard as you can for the first half of your life and do whatever is necessary to get ahead and make a killing. Then at half time, at the break (age fifty, let's say), you reflect and come back in the second half and give away your time to others and to whatever God you obey. The balance is perfect and the intention good, but the notion of "halves" is deeply misleading. Why not wait until the last two minutes in this game of life or to your last breath and make some plea for salvation, so as to give something back in your will?

This is fake generosity. God doesn't want a half of your life or a half of your money or a half of anything. He wants it all: all the time, every day, every hour, every minute, and every second. Half time is a heresy. The amount of time and effort we expend on God's work and on our calling is not a trivial thing. As John Calvin suggested in his still renowned *Institutes of the Christian Religion,* intimated nearly five hundred years ago during the Reformation, "we are all ministers."[3] The priesthood of believers means the laity is asked, indeed expected, to take up the cross and follow Christ, wherever it takes them. Everyone, not just clergy, is in the ministry, and not half the time.

In this respect we should never forget that time and death present us with a unique opportunity for giving. In *The Fable of the Bees*, a work of satirical social comment and profound economic theory published in 1705, Bernard Mandeville damns with ironical praise the great benefactor of Oxford and its university, Dr. John Radcliffe.[4] After a life of exemplary miserliness, Radcliffe added to the distress of his relatives by leaving nothing to them in his will and rewarding no one for the affection that he had undeservedly received. Instead he bestowed the entire legacy on Oxford in exchange for the immortalization of his name in the "Radcliffe Infirmary," the "Radcliffe Camera," and so on. Mandeville's book is subtitled *Private Vices, Publick Benefits*, and he takes Radcliffe as an example of the way in which—by the "invisible hand" that Adam Smith was later to extol as the prime mover of a free economy—self-interested actions can contribute, in a free economy, to the public good.

Most people would agree with Mandeville that Radcliffe was the opposite of generous. Not because he gave no money away—he did give it away, the whole lot. What he did not give away, however, was his own time and energy, which were devoted entirely to himself and to accumulat-

Johann Sebastian Bach
(1685–1750)

 THE PROLIFIC GERMAN composer and organist defines the Baroque era in works for choir, orchestra, and solo instruments. Bach's works are revered for their intellectual depth and technical and artistic beauty. Bach was educated at St. Michel's School in Luneburg. He became a concert musician in the chapel of Duke Johann Ernst in Weimar and later, Amstadt. He took time off to visit Buxtehude, the father of German organ music by whom he was influenced. He married his second cousin and had seven children. Bach had been an organist at Muhlhausen for only a year when he left the post to be organist and concertmaster at the ducal court in Weimar. There he was very productive in composing. He then moved to Cothen to be director of music for Prince Leopold. His wife died, and he remarried to a much younger woman. They had thirteen more children, only six of whom survived to adulthood. Bach spent his midlife in Leipzig as cantor, where he directed students and composed. In 1847 he was asked to the court of Frederick II in Prussia, where he published and perfected *The Art of Fugue.*

Bach's musical style arose from his extraordinary fluency in contrapuntal invention and motivic control; his flair for improvisation at the keyboard; his exposure to South German, North German, Italian, and French music; and his devotion to the Lutheran liturgy. Bach gave both time and energy to the following: his wife Anna Magdalena,

(*continues*)

whose musical education he took in hand with the wonderful *Notebook* for her; his many children—having so many was already an act of huge generosity, ensuring that they in turn became distinguished composers (and indeed the most distinguished of their day in the case of two) a further huge act of generosity, given what else Bach could have done with his time; the outpouring of compositions, the readiness to produce a new cantata every Sunday and not take shortcuts, the readiness too with a musical gift whenever appropriate, and—with his musical offering to Frederick the Great—a gift for mankind and not just for the monarch. His is real generosity, though not involving money.

ing property for his own use during his lifetime. Never did others become objects of his charity, and even the posthumous gift to Oxford was a gift to himself—the last thing he could do to perpetuate his name and receive enduring honor.

In short it is only when we devote our *time on earth* to others that we make genuine gifts, and it is for this reason that the use of time is such an important part of generosity—more important than the use of wealth. The moment of time, this moment, this very second, not some far-off future or a coming Sunday in a pew, is also a time that God wants our devotion. Jimmy Carter was once ridiculed for saying he prayed all the time. But that is what 1 Thessalonians 5:17 demands: "Pray without ceasing." Travelers in Muslim countries are often moved by the sight of a society in which all people, regardless of occupation, rank, age, or sex, are called five times a day from the minaret to leave off everything and to prostrate themselves in prayer. This entirely transforms the sense of time in a Muslim community: time is allotted by the voice of the muezzin, and is understood instinctively as a gift from God, which must in turn be given to him. A well-known Harvard theologian likewise compared prayer to the act of breathing. In every breath, in and out, God is with you, when you place yourself in his trust.

It is not only time and wealth that we are called upon to give. Our talents too are ours to use and to use for others. Giving of talent is not like performing in a talent show in which you put yourself on display, seeking admiration. It is an act performed for others' sake. Many people think they have talent merely because they have some party trick that will attract an audience. But the real talent is the one that brings another kind of return.

The "talent" in the ancient world was a measure or unit of mass: one foot cubed. For the Romans, a talent weighed one hundred libra (pounds). The same measure was often applied to the weight of gold and silver. In the New Testament, in Jesus' parable of the Talents (Matt. 25:14–30), the talent is coinage—representing a large sum of money. The parable tells the story of gifts or skills that were invested, as opposed to being wasted. Doing nothing with them was, it turns out, worse than attempting something and failing. The meanings of this parable are many. One is that God wants us to take a risk with our coins and also with our gifts and skills. Only in risk is there any chance for reward.

We live in a time in which people are increasingly encouraged to transfer the risks of living to others. Our hunter-gatherer ancestors had to risk their lives, their comforts, and their health in order to supply food to their families and their tribes. Many of us today have become dependent on others to take those risks on our behalf, and many also look to the state to regulate and confine our lives in such a way that risk is no longer a day-to-day reality. Yet we need risks, not merely in order to enjoy the benefits of a free economy, but also in order to grow as human beings and to offer what we have to others. In our risk-averse society, it is a rare sight when someone risks his life to save another or risks his wealth to help others, as Muhammad Yunus did in establishing the Grameen Bank. The virtues of courage, prudence, and temperance all involve exposing ourselves to risks and facing them down.

Justice, kindness, and generosity also demand a cheerful and risk-taking spirit. Giving is a risky business, as is any action that creates a relation with another human being. Those who prefer safety are unlikely to go out to others in the spontaneous way that generosity requires. "Being careful" is another name for meanness.

In fact, the greatest gifts are those that put the giver at risk. As Christ himself said (and also exemplified): "Greater love hath no man than this, that a man lay down his life for his friend" (John 15:13). The greatest gifts are those that entail sacrifice that deprive the giver of something he wants or needs, including, perhaps, life itself. In wartime and times of crisis, people understand this more fully. They are constantly being confronted with acts of heroism in which one person gives everything to those in his or her charge, like the officer who falls on a grenade to protect his troops, or the person who enters a burning building to rescue those inside. We saw some of this kind of heroism displayed by the city fire brigades of New York, during the dreadful events of 9/11. And the spectacle of their sacrifice had a transforming effect on those who

Felix Mendelssohn
(1809–47)

THE GERMAN COMPOSER, pianist, and conductor from the Romantic era was born in Hamburg into a prominent Jewish banking family. His creative genius is recognized for his symphonies, concerti, oratorios, and piano and chamber music. Moving to Berlin, Mendelssohn is often thought to be the greatest child prodigy after Mozart. He also mastered languages and classical literature. After university he composed and performed, later being elevated to be conductor of the Leipzig Gewandhaus Orchestra. Married to Cecile, they had five children and a very happy marriage. The conservative strain of his music set him apart from other more flamboyant contemporaries. His success, popularity, and Jewish background irked Richard Wagner, and during the Nazi regime his music was banned. Mendelssohn is generous not in giving away money to charity, but that he gave time and energy to things other than his own composing—most importantly, to reviving the music of Bach and making it available to the public, to the Leipzig Gewandhaus and its orchestra, and to the cause of German music, all of which he did with superb grace and public spirit.

witnessed it. Suddenly they were presented with the proof that life is worthwhile—worthwhile because it is a gift that can in turn be given.

Therefore, as you think about becoming a better steward, do not think only in monetary terms. Money is not the only thing we have to give. It's not even the most important thing. Consider also your gifts of time and talent and how they can be used to serve others. Pray and work to develop the courage to take risks and to make sacrifices for the good of others. I believe that in doing so, you will unlock to the doors to contentment and joy. Stewardship is not some Faustian bargain or a form of long-term hedonism directed to the happy afterlife. It is nothing more than a "living" faith, here and now, next door, across the nation and around the globe.

Generosity and Economics 5

*The Rich must live more simply so that
the Poor may simply live.*

MAHATMA GANDHI

SUPPLY MEETS DEMAND; demand matches supply. Economics is all about the intersection of these two crucial curves. "Supply-Demand" describes relations between buyers and sellers of any good or service. The model determines prices and quantity sold in a given market. In a competitive market, prices function to equalize the quantity demanded by consumers and the quantity supplied by producers, resulting in an economic equilibrium. Where and how does generosity fit into the equation? Or does it?

Herbert Gintis of the University of Massachusetts, a self-described former Marxist economist, is among the few economists to address the matter of economics and generosity. Gintis is codirector of the Preference Network team. His team's research, among other things, is dispelling the myth of happy generous savages who are corrupted by contact with markets and modern societies. It turns out that the more "savages" actually participate in markets, the more generous and filled with apparent "fellow feeling" they tend to be.

Based on his research, Gintis believes that history traces humanity's rise from tribal selfishness to more cosmopolitan liberality. He says, "Market societies give rise to more egalitarianism and movements toward democracy, civil liberties, and civil rights." He points out, "Market societies and democratic societies are practically co-extensive."[1] And it appears they are more generous too.

Gintis speculates that markets bring strangers into contact on a regular basis, encouraging people to develop more concern for others beyond their family and immediate neighbors. Instead of parochialism, being integrated into markets encourages a spirit of ecumenism.

In a classic treatment of this subject, the book *Generosity: Virtue in the Civil Society* by the libertarian economic-philosopher Tibor Machan both makes a case for generosity as a "civic virtue" and denies that law can enjoin it.[2] Grounding his arguments in a rational-egoistic, natural-law-based "virtue ethic," he presents what may be the best argument to date that the virtue of generosity is a constitutive part of a well-lived human life. He then proceeds to demolish the view that generosity may properly, or can effectively, be enforced by a "welfare state."

Economics and Morality

One of the first principles of economics suggests that material prosperity depends upon moral convictions and moral dealings. You might say you never heard *economics* and *moral* in the same sentence and that it sounds like an oxymoron. Adam Smith, the principal founder of economic science in the eighteenth century, was himself a professor

J. C. Penney
(1875–1971)

THIS CHAIN STORE executive was a pioneer in profit sharing as well as a major philanthropist. He built an empire based on the precepts of the Golden Rule. Born in Hamilton, Missouri, as the seventh of twelve children, his beginnings were poor. His father, Rev. James Cash Penney Sr., was an unpaid pastor in the Primitive Baptist church who earned a living raising pigs and selling watermelons. J. C. Penney Jr. moved to Colorado and was employed in a merchants dry goods store chain. Married for twenty-eight years, he lived very frugally and started his own store chain. In time there were 1,660 stores with sales over $4 billion, making it second only to Sears Roebuck & Company in nonfood retailers in the country. Some fifty thousand employees, or "associates" as he called them, shared in all the profits. His charitable giving was to religious endeavors, including the YMCA, 4-H, Boy Scouts, and Allied Youth. While he had no college education, Penney received seventeen honorary degrees and many other awards. In the crash of 1929 he lost $40 million, but started over again. Faith in God and country were his cardinal principles.

of moral philosophy. He took it for granted that moral beliefs should and do affect economics. The success of economic measures, like the success of most other things in human existence, depends upon certain moral habits. If those habits are lacking, the only other way to produce goods is by compulsion—by what is called slave labor. Let us examine briefly some of the moral qualities that make possible a prosperous economy, as there is a strong connection to being generous.

Any economy that functions well relies upon a high degree of honesty. Of course, some "bad apples"—cheats and charlatans—can be found in any society. Yet on the whole, in a prospering economy most people behave honestly. Echoing an old English proverb, Benjamin Franklin wrote in the eighteenth-century *Almanacs* he penned in Philadelphia, "Honesty is the best policy." He meant that, in an economic sense, honesty pays.

All advanced economies are based on contracts: agreements to sell or to buy, promises to pay, deeds of sale, all sorts of "commercial instruments." Many commercial contracts are oral, rather than written. Today's markets especially depend on implied contracts (as distinguished from detailed written and signed contracts). In public auctions bidders may pledge a large sum of money merely by raising one hand or nodding their heads. The auctioneer trusts the bidder to keep his promise to buy at a certain price. On a much vaster scale, the complex apparatus of stock markets depends on such implicit contracts—and on ordinary honesty. This can also be seen as the duty of "good faith," which is implied in every commercial contract and set in uniform commercial codes.

On the other hand, those societies in which theft, cheating, corruption, and lying are common do not ordinarily develop successful economies. If production and distribution can be carried on only under armed protectors and without any certainty of being paid, then little will be produced and distributed above the level of subsistence. When bargains are not kept and loans are not repaid, prices are high and interest rates are higher, which discourages production and distribution. This is the opposite of what you want.

Another moral quality or habit important for the success of an economy is the custom of doing good work—of producing goods or offering services of high quality. The Romans had a word for this: *industria*, a moral virtue, from which our English word "industry" is itself derived. Goods should be produced, and services rendered, for the sake of turning out something satisfactory or even admirable—not for the sake merely of cash payment. This affection for quality is bound up with the hope of pleasing or helping the purchaser or customer: doing something kindly for other people, even though producer and distributor may never see most of the customers.

This belief in working faithfully and well is connected with the virtue called charity. For charity is not a handout; primarily as we have seen, the word means "tenderness or love, affection for other people." The producer who creates first-rate goods is serving other people and can take satisfaction in that service. Charity should not be "crowded out," as the economists put it, by the state.

Still another moral virtue of the marketplace is a kind of courage, what the Romans used to call *fortitude*. This economic courage includes the willingness to take risks, the ability to endure hard times, the talent to hold out against all the disappointment, harassment, ingratitude, and folly that fall upon people in the world of getting and spending. As I have already argued, there is a deep connection between generosity and risk-taking—a connection that goes to the heart of our nature as practical and social beings.

It would be easy enough to list other moral beliefs and customs that contribute to the foundation of a prosperous economy, but I have made my point. So instead let us turn to a discussion of the vice of envy and of its opposite, the virtue of generosity. Envy is a sour emotion that condemns a person to loneliness. It means coveting what is not yours. Generosity is an emotion that attracts friends. The generous man or woman is always ready to praise others sincerely and to help them instead of hindering them. Generosity brings admiration of the achievements and qualities of other people. Generous relations beget more generosity in a circle of virtue.

Now generosity, too, is a moral quality on which a sound economy depends. Producer and distributor, when they are moved by generosity, do not envy one another: they may be competitors, but they are friendly competitors, like contestants in a sport. And in a society with a strong element of generosity, most citizens do not support public measures that would pull down or repress the more productive and energetic and ingenious, enterprising individuals.

Generosity and Economic Systems

A spirit of generosity toward others is still at work in America and elsewhere. But in much of the world, a very different spirit has unfortunately come to prevail. In socialist-inspired lands, envy is the rule, approved by those in power. Private wealth and personal success are

John Walton
(1946–2005)

JOHN IS the late son of the legendary Wal-Mart founder, Sam Walton. He inherited his vast fortune with other family members. Their family foundation focuses on education in the United States. He donated $1 billion to charitable funds in his lifetime. As chairman of the venture capital firm True North, Walton also wanted to see a more enterprising spirit in philanthropy. He was a Green Beret in Vietnam and had a tenacious attitude to life. He worked to establish a Children's Scholarship Fund to help low-income families get the best private school education. He was also an advocate of school vouchers. John died prematurely in a plane crash. His net worth was $18.2 billion, the fourth richest in the U.S., and his survivors are continuing in his established spirit of giving.

denounced on principle. The Marxist indoctrinator deliberately preaches envy. By appealing to that strong vice, he may be able to pull down constitutions, classes, and religions. Socialism is lavish with other people's money and posits an overbearing welfare state to serve as a pseudo-nanny, deliberately stealing from the rich in order to benefit the poor, and especially those who don't care to work or contribute to society. This lavishness is not generosity, since it is expressly designed to remake society so that gift will no longer be either necessary or attractive. The socialist society is one in which we are given nothing, but take everything as a "right." As I argued in chapter 3, this is the formula for a society without gratitude, and one in which risk-aversion and meanness bring about a steady demoralization of the people as a whole.

We can see evidence of this when we compare the statistics concerning giving and volunteering in the relatively free economy of the United States with those of the welfare economies of Europe. In 2007, over $290 billion was given to U.S. charities, with $199 billion (77 percent) of this given by individuals. The absolute amount of charitable giving is not only high, but the proportion of income donated has grown. In 1954, the average individual in the U.S. gave 1.9 percent of after-tax income to charity ($222), while in 2007 giving averaged 2.2 percent of after-tax income ($656, inflation adjusted). In 2007, approximately one-third of this giving was directed to religious organizations, followed by 19 percent to health and human wellbeing. In 2007, over sixty-five million Americans volunteered to help charities. Ninety-six percent of volunteers said that one of their motivations was "feeling compassion toward other people."

In the midst of all this giving, the physiologic mechanisms that support altruism and generosity are little understood. Human beings routinely help strangers at costs to themselves, and in a free economy this disposition to offer relief to the stranger seems to be far greater than in economies where relief is regarded as the concern of the state.

Thus charitable giving in the U.S., which amounts to 1.7

percent of GDP, is twelve times greater than charitable giving in France (0.14 percent of GDP). France has the most statist of the European economies, with over half of all employees being employed by the state, and over half of GNP being produced by the state. Britain, whose economy is as free as the postwar socialist consensus has allowed any European economy to be, is situated between the U.S. and France, with 0.73 percent of GDP accounted for by charity. Equally significant are the statistics for Germany, in which the former West Germany, where the vestiges of a free economy have survived the social democratic consensus, spends 0.26 percent of GDP on charitable giving, while the former East Germany, still mired in the collective resentment instilled and exploited by communism, spends a mere 0.12 percent.

By the same token, giving tends to represent a lower proportion of GDP in countries with higher levels of personal taxation, since high taxation is always justified by the pretense that the state is "looking after" those compelled to pay it. The "social sector," as Peter Drucker named it, today accounts for almost a third of U.S. GNP, and it has been growing, so it cannot be dismissed as a passing fashion. Being generous is part of the economics of a free society, as well as a core component in the bonds of citizenship. The rest of the world needs to wake up to what we in America have discovered, namely that a free civil society is more likely to offer help to those in need than a welfare state organized on socialist principles. Not only that, but the gentle but effective bond of gift, which holds society together without threatening its freedom, is more likely to arise where the state retreats from the center of things than in conditions of centralized control. As we see today in Burma and North Korea, states that control things also prevent things. And the spontaneous desires of good people everywhere to do what they can to avert famine in North Korea and, in the aftermath of the 2008 cyclone, starvation and disease in Burma are frustrated by the greatest enemies of generosity, which are the centralized state and free citizenship.

It is safe to conclude that only when people are free to give are they able to give, and only in a free economy do they gain the means to give generously. I argued earlier that governments are poor at generosity because they use other people's money and have no appreciation for either earning it or stewarding it. Government generosity is truly an oxymoron, and the politicians who claim to practice it are usually the biggest fakes, people who demonstrate none of the virtue in their personal lives, which also makes them hypocrites.

When individuals compete to give more, everyone benefits. And only in a system that separates societal institutions is there maximum freedom. When tax laws encourage charitable donations and permit them to flow to places of choice, there is an opportunity for maximum giving, the commencement of charitable foundations, and the formation of the most generous kinds of society. In such free societies, be it the U.S. or anywhere else (and hopefully more and more as we move to a global civilization with the emergence of civil societies everywhere), we are gaining an appreciation for what the wise nineteenth-century prime minister of the Netherlands, Abraham Kuyper, called "sphere sovereignty."[3]

What Kuyper meant by this combination of words is that democratic capitalism is best conducted under a theory of society that appreciates the sovereignty of God

Henry Ford
(1863–1947)

FORD DID NOT believe in charity. He is famous for founding the Ford Motor Company and was generous with his money. His desire was to help people find a place where they never needed charity. As a pioneer in the automotive industry, his reputation became legend. He was also a generous employer in both hourly pay and benefits. He established schools, housing for the needy, orphanages, hospitals, and museums. His son, Edsel, established the Ford Foundation in 1936. The first gifts went largely to Detroit area charities. He left 90 percent of company stock to the foundation. Over time, the giving became more liberal and Henry Ford II resigned from the board in protest in 1977. He criticized the lack of interest and support for free enterprise. Today, the Ford Foundation is one of the world's largest foundations with well over $10 billion in assets.

and respects the authority of each domain: the economy (businesses), the family, the church, the school, voluntary associations, and the public sphere of politics and governmental action. Sphere sovereignty implied that no one area of life or social community should dictate or be sovereign over the other. Each had its own integrity. Sphere sovereignty is a better alternative to the worldviews of both ecclesiasticism (or theocracy) and secularism (or any other form of statist philosophy).

Kuyper based his thinking on the understanding of *Coram Deo*—the Reformed Church doctrine that requires that every part of life be lived directly "before the face of God." The separation of church and state should result, he thought, in the separation of the state from all the other societal spheres. Kuyper's philosophy was principally anti-statist, though he upheld the right and duty of government to establish justice in the public sphere. His theory was much more than a theory: it was the operating system for his own and other countries for nearly a century and a half. A free society allows not only the greatest measure of freedom in each of its spheres but also the greatest opportunity for generosity.

In his book *Who Really Cares: America's Charity Divide, Who Gives, Who Doesn't and Why It Matters*, Arthur Brooks, a behavioral economist at the Maxwell School at Syracuse University and at the American Enterprise Institute (AEI), finds that America has two nations: givers and nongivers.[4] He was surprised by his own findings, namely, that three-quarters of all Americans give their time and money to various charities, churches, and causes, while the other quarter does not. His research demonstrates that self-described conservatives are actually much more compassionate than their liberal foes. This too surprised many people. What, you might ask, correlates most highly with strong giving? Brooks' answer from the vast amount of data shows that strong families, church attendance, earned (as opposed to state-subsidized) income, and belief in indi-

Eli Lilly
(1838–98)

BORN IN BALTIMORE, Maryland, Lilly became a leading manufacturer of legal drugs as well as a philanthropist. A chemist by training, he opened his first drugstore in 1860. After serving in the Civil War as a colonel in the cavalry, he returned to the manufacturing of pharmaceuticals in Indianapolis, where his company became one of the largest drug makers in the United States. Demonstrating his public spiritedness, Lilly founded Consumers Gas Trust and a public water company. He also participated in many civic duties. His Indianapolis "Plan of Relief" became a model for helping the unemployed. His family, at his bequest, started an endowment charity in 1937, made possible through vast amounts of gifts of stock in the company. The main causes over the decades have included religion, education, and economic development.

viduals not governments determine how likely one is to give. Charity is a big number in the U.S. economy and it is growing, so it matters not just to individuals who give and who receive it but also to the nation as a whole. If you removed the charity number and the voluntary component monetized in time given away from the present economy, we would witness a dramatic downturn in economic prospects and overall performance.

In sum, when it comes to economics, giving matters. It matters greatly, and not for individuals only. It matters for the whole social organism of which individuals are a part.

Generosity and Science 6

The habit of giving only enhances the desire to give.

WALT WHITMAN

PAUL ZAK, an economics professor at Claremont Graduate University (who I predict could win a Nobel Prize for this), and his coworkers, Angela Stanton at Chapman University and Sheila Ahmadi at UCLA Geffen School of Medicine, have found that injecting people with oxytocin makes them more generous. Oxytocin is the hormone that enhances attachment between sexual partners and also between mothers and their children. It has the effect of "opening" people to attachment in circumstances where bonding is a beneficial response.

It is not surprising that Zak and his colleagues have uncovered a link between oxytocin and generosity.[1] Their research shows that human beings routinely help strangers at costs to themselves. Sometimes the help offered is generous—offering more than the other expects. The proximate mechanisms supporting generosity however are not well understood. In Zak et al.'s study, participants were infused with either 40 IU oxytocin (OT) or a placebo and then engaged in a blinded, one-shot decision on how to split a sum of money with a stranger. Those on OT were 80 percent more generous than those who'd been given a placebo. OT had no effect on a unilateral monetary transfer task dissociating generosity from altruism. OT and altruism together predicted almost half the interpersonal variation in generosity. Notably, OT had a twofold larger impact on generosity compared to altruism.

The upshot of this somewhat technical analysis is that the research suggests that generosity is a disposition that goes beyond our species-based tendency to altruistic behavior. It connects with the biological roots of more personal loves —the loves that attach us to others and lead us to care for them as individuals.

Martin Nowak, who was formerly in the zoology department at Oxford and is now at Harvard in mathematics and biology, builds on the earlier work of people such as Robert Axelrod on what is called "tit for tat" strategies in game theory. Nowak's findings are collected in his award-winning book on cooperation, *Evolutionary Dynamics*.[2] Nowak's latest research, popularized in both *Science* and *Nature* magazines and covered broadly in the press, suggests that it pays to be "more generous," at least in the prisoner dilemma games he studies.

Nowak is busy creating a new field called, as with the title of his book, "evolutionary dynamics," wherein Darwin's natural selection is formulated in terms of mathematical equations. He is out to prove that cooperation is a more successful genetic strategy than selfishness and that forgiveness is, from a pragmatic point of view, more successful than tit for tat. Hence the social virtues will emerge over time as "evolutionarily stable strategies" of the organisms that possess them. Life is all about cooperation.

Jeffrey Skoll
(1965–)

As EBAY'S FIRST president, Skoll prospered early in life. He retired at age thirty-four and used $34 million from the proceeds of the company's IPO to set up his own foundation. As one of the youngest philanthropists in U.S. history, his major emphasis is entrepreneurial projects. His giving mirrors that of a venture capital firm. A $7.5 million gift to Oxford University to integrate social entrepreneurship into business skills is indicative of his visionary interests. He is now financing and producing films on social responsibility. The Skoll Foundation, established in 1999, pursues his vision of a world "where all people, regardless of geography, background, or economic status enjoy and employ the full range of their talents and abilities." Skoll is looking to lead lasting social change. He invests in social entrepreneurship through his flagship awards program. He connects people through a center at Saïd Business School. He sponsors forums with top thinkers and has built Social Edge as an online community where like-minded people can network, learn, and inspire one another.

In other words, Nowak's research shows that human beings are natural cooperators who choose generosity over greed and forgiveness over revenge or retaliation. As one headline put it, "'Give and ye shall receive' is not the Gospel but Darwin." Nowak has shown that the motor that drives evolution and the survival of our species is altruism. Generosity is the link to cooperation, perhaps not just in the lab or in scientific experiments but in the real world as well.

Nowak's results are confirmed by the extensive empirical work of zoologist Frans de Waal and his team at Emory University in their observations of primate societies.[3] The evidence of de Waal shows that species such as monkeys and apes incur a cost to help others. Clearly these species do not have the cognitive machinery that humans have. They cannot understand fully the consequences of their actions. Yet de Waal's studies demonstrate that such animals have strategies both to enforce fairness and to punish those who try to take a free ride or break the governing rules. Based on this field of science, scientists have discovered that the motivation in humans to cooperate is rather ancient. They think that generosity is, for instance, embedded in human nature. Generosity may very well be hardwired into our brains.

Of course, generosity of this kind is to be seen largely in the context of conflict resolution and social cooperation. As such, it confers a benefit, both on the genes of individuals and on the society to which they belong. Human generosity has another dimension, a dimension of sacrificial love that quite transcends anything that could motivate an animal, since it is based on the consideration of the "Other" as a free being whose interests take precedence over mine. This human generosity points the way to another, more perfect state than the peace of bonobos or the domestic bliss of gorillas.

Stephen Post of Stony Brook University has done years of research showing that generosity is the key to happiness.

John Templeton
(1912–2008)

A PIONEER in financial investments, the Tennessee native became a full-time philanthropist later in life. Templeton started on Wall Street in 1937 after graduating from Yale and becoming a Rhodes scholar. He ran some of the world's largest and most successful international mutual funds. He was called the "global stock picker of the century." He sold his company in 1992 to the Franklin Group for $440 million. A naturalized citizen of the Bahamas, he was knighted in 1987. His foundation awards the richest (£1 million annual) prize on "Progress Toward Research on Discoveries about Spiritual Realities." The John Templeton Foundation, now based outside of Philadelphia, grants millions of dollars a year to various projects, college courses, books, essays, and scientific research on the benefits of cooperation between science and religion and on answers to the "really big questions." Presbyterian by upbringing, Templeton was a church elder and a trustee on the board of Princeton Theological Seminary. He was also involved in the American Bible Society. He espoused a "humble approach" to theology and tried to increase a hundredfold spiritual information to supplement the ancient scriptures of all religions. He had a special interest in the topics of forgiveness, thrift, character development, and altruism. As the author of many titles on the laws of life and generosity, Templeton has been called "the most generous soul in the world."

His body of work demonstrates that being generous and giving freely allows one to be measurably happier.

The universal quest for happiness may not be too difficult after all. For Aristotle, philanthropy is "friendship love," or *philia*, which is the very basis of community. Just take the money or time you would have otherwise spent on things you don't need and spend it instead generously on others. These are the clear findings from this new school called "positive psychology." Post and others from this school demonstrate that giving is the real key to feeling happy. Generosity brings more happiness than selfish indulgence. Those who give live longer, are healthier, and are far happier than their counterparts. Post's research gives some teeth to the motherly admonition that it is better to give than to receive. He and his colleagues have the hard research in psychology and biology that back it up. To quote him, "Statistical analysis revealed that personal spending had no link with a person's happiness, while spending on others and charity was significantly related to a boost in happiness."

The Institute for Research on Unlimited Love, founded by Post, has funded and directed over five hundred scientific studies to date that demonstrate the power of unselfish love. In his best-selling book, *Why Good Things Happen to Good People*, Post summarizes years of scientific research and identifies ways of giving that contribute to mental and physical health.[4]

In sum, being generous—giving to others without expecting anything in return—is not just the right thing to do. It's also a very practical thing for those who want to feel healthier, be happier, and live longer. More and more this conclusion is being demonstrated not merely as an optimistic idea, but as scientific fact.

Responsible Generosity 7

Before you finish eating breakfast in the morning,
you've depended on more than half the world.
This is the way our universe is structured;
this is its interrelated quality.

MARTIN LUTHER KING JR.

THE OVERARCHING PURPOSE of this book is to encourage the embracing of generosity as a virtue. However, the mere desire to be generous is sometimes not enough if the goal is to truly help others.

The truth is that generosity can be a fool's game. Both at home and abroad, its path is sometimes lined with traps and snares. Philanthropic generosity can be misguided or even counterproductive. It is subject to institutional abuse. The megafailures of aid to the Less Developed Countries over five decades, the War on Poverty, and similar large government programs have been sufficiently documented, so much so that we do not need to recite the conclusions. The argument and data presented by former World Bank economist William Easterly in *The White Man's Burden* clearly demonstrate that billions upon billions of dollars over several decades have been wasted in the development game.[1]

But there is even darker stuff, if the total truth is known. In *Silent Accomplice*, journalist Andrew Wallis speaks openly for the first time about the French and Rwanda, describing how philanthropy paid for PR to cover up the deep support for mass genocide.[2] And the classic, eye-opening account in *The Road to Hell* exposed the aid industry itself as a big business concerned more with winning the next contract than with actually helping needy people.[3]

Many people care deeply about bringing hope and help to poverty-stricken areas of the developing world or to American ghettos. But often the best actions of these idealists, though rooted in a desire to be generous, are inadvertently destructive, thanks to a combination of gross naiveté and a willingness of native elites to exploit them. The underscrutinization of aid effectiveness, cost structures, overhead, and performance track records is almost enough to lead sincere and willing donors to just throw up their hands in disgust and utter confusion. Responsible generosity requires that gifts be used well or, at the very least, do no harm. As Carnegie himself taught in his *Gospel of Wealth*, in bestowing charity, the main consideration should be to help those who are willing to help themselves. He believed almsgiving can do more harm or injury performed by rewarding vice than by relieving virtue. C. S. Lewis likewise also once recanted that the proper aim of giving is surely to "put the recipient in a state where he no longer needs our gift."

If Easterly is correct—and I believe he is—then aid (and especially aid from governments and international bodies such as the World Bank and UN agencies) can sometimes be worse than the disease it was supposed to cure. The data sets collected by Sala-i-Martin, a research professor at Columbia University, show the same effects. They conclude that economies can, over the long term, be hurt by aid on which they become dependent. His data show that successful economic development is spurred by local cultures and enterprise more than by outright gifts. The story of so-called "helpful aid" in India by Gurcharan Das, in *India Unbound*, is another example of a sorry state of affairs that led to underdevelopment and socialism in India lasting for more than four decades.[4]

Responsible generosity consists of more than mere good intentions. It steers clear of careless strategies or ideologically motivated theories. It includes a willingness to follow through, to examine the results of the charitable giving. It takes full responsibility for the use of the donated resources. In short, responsibility must be viewed as a sort of subspecies of stewardship. For if there is one lesson on generosity to learn from global experience in the post–World War II period, it may be that even the most entrepreneurial wealth creators need to give more careful attention to the execution of entrepreneurialism in their giving in order for it to be effective.

Positive Signs

Today around the globe there can be found increasing efforts to define and enact more generous societies. The government in the United Kingdom recently initiated a new campaign, which it has called "A Generous Society." Philanthropy is regaining popularity and heft in the U.K. after decades of disuse as society searches for new ways to fund its social outreach programs. The National Giving Campaign concluded in its final report, "A Blueprint for Giving," that "there is no single big idea that will dramatically change the culture of giving in the UK" and that "the way forward lies with a set of targeted initiatives." It also threw down the challenge to double charitable donations in real terms over the next ten years.

The Gordon Brown administration has agreed with this analysis and has committed to playing its part in meeting the campaign's challenge. "A Generous Society" sets out the government's plans to:

- work with young people so that the culture of giving is instilled at an early age;
- work with employers and employees so that existing schemes like payroll giving and gifts of shares are maximized and so that new approaches to social investment are fostered;
- work with charities to promote tax-efficient giving so that they get the full benefit of existing and new schemes; and
- work in partnership with a wide range of stakeholders to extend opportunities to give across society.

This seems like a good plan to get giving back on track in Britain. After all, in Victorian times, England, Scotland, and Wales were charitable and generous societies. Only after a century of state-oriented socialism has it become apparent that something was lacking. What was lacking? As previously noted, the culture of gift, in which good things are received with gratitude and not as "rights," was missing. It is this culture that the nanny state destroys, and if people have been slow to wake up to this fact, it is partly because the therapeutic state brings with it the vested interests of people whose jobs depend on organizing a society on principles other than those of gift.

John D. Rockefeller
(1839–1937)

ROCKEFELLER WAS PERHAPS the leading American industrialist and philanthropist of his era. He revolutionized the oil industry and came to define modern philanthropy. He founded Standard Oil Company as an Ohio partnership. He became in short order the world's richest man and the first billionaire. He spent forty years doing philanthropy targeted on medicine, education, and scientific research. As a Northern Baptist, he supported many church-based institutions and charities. Religiously tithing 10 percent of his pay to church and religious work, Rockefeller was keen to develop a model and pattern for giving. A large gift helped the all-black Spelman College thrive, and an $80 million gift to the University of Chicago in 1900 made it a world-class institution.

Passionaries: Turning Compassion into Action tells the stories of some thirty-five individuals who transformed their compassion into positive actions that significantly changed the lives of others.[5] What all have in common is a sense of being generous. Each person asked, "How can I make a difference?" The tales they relate are those of social entrepreneurs turning who they are into action with surprising effect. Americans have long wanted to change the world, create a legacy, make a mark, and leave the world a better place. These "moderate heroes" show how they did it. You can't help but be encouraged to join the ranks of the more than twenty-five million Americans who volunteer, who give their time and talent to help others and to build organizations that change society for the good.

Marc Freedman is the founder and CEO of Civic Ventures in San Francisco, which was formed to help expand the contributions of older persons. He is working to change the face of retirement. His book *Encore: Finding Work That Matters in the Second Half of Life* explains why people in their fifties and sixties and beyond need "productive relationships" in pursuit of a larger good.[6] Studies show that today people want and often need to work longer, beyond the age at which earlier generations retired. Frequently these "encore" individuals seek an opportunity to do what they have always wanted to do. They engage themselves in volunteer work and often look for fundamental aspiration. They want to use their life experience in valuable ways. A new phase of work comes about, one that balances fulfillment and giving back against getting paid less so as to accomplish something greater. Older Americans are not just living improved lives in terms of longevity and independence. They now see a challenge of giving through purposeful employment that entails a chance to contribute to society in the twenty-first century.

Another example of generosity taking off and gaining acceptance in the larger, popular culture is *Oprah's Big Give,* an exciting primetime series that defied television convention with the bold idea of people competing to give rather than get. It premiered on the ABC television network in the spring of 2008.

In eight one-hour episodes, a diverse, determined, and competitive group of ten people were given the challenge of a lifetime—to change the lives of complete strangers in the most creative and dramatic ways. In this intense competition, the contestants criss-crossed the country, scrambling to find ways to impact the fates and fortunes of unsuspecting people who were in for the surprise of their lives. Lives were changed in the blink of an eye as contestants raced against time to create once-in-a-lifetime experiences and also to give away hundreds of thousands of dollars.

In the final analysis, regardless of TV shows and government campaigns, a sympathetic community of fellow feeling and generous persons who abhor the pain and suffering of other persons and who aspire to do good is the very basis of our free market economy and the kind of democratic society it engenders. This is not the self-interested, profit-making-at-all costs euphemism that the media has urged on us, redefining capitalism as greed. Rather, other-interest and generosity are the twin engines of a healthy free market and a generous society.

TOMS Shoes is another interesting movement rooted in generosity. It was started on a simple premise: for every pair of shoes purchased, TOMS will *give* a pair of shoes to a child in need. Using the purchasing power of individuals to benefit the greater good is what the company is all about.

In 2006, an American traveler, Blake Mycoskie, befriended children in Argentina and found they had no shoes to protect their feet. Wanting to help, he created a company that would match every pair of shoes sold with a pair given to a child in need. He called this idea "One for One." Since its inception, TOMS has given more than 140,000 pairs of shoes to children in need through its model. Because of customer support, TOMS plans to give more than 300,000 pairs of shoes to children in need around the world in 2009.

You may ask, "Why shoes?" Most children in developing countries grow up barefoot. Whether at play, doing chores, or just getting around, these children are at risk. Walking is often the primary mode of transportation in developing countries. Children can walk for miles to get food, water, shelter, and medical help. Wearing shoes enables them to walk distances that are not possible when barefoot, as without shoes they are susceptible to getting cuts and sores on unsafe roads and from contaminated soil. Not only are these injuries painful, they also are dangerous when wounds become infected. The leading cause of disease in developing countries is soil-transmitted parasites, which penetrate the skin through open sores. Wearing shoes can often prevent this and the risk of amputation.

Often, children cannot attend school barefoot because shoes are a required part of their uniform. If they do not have shoes, they do not go to school. If they do not receive an education, they do not have the opportunity to realize their real potential. TOMS Shoes' simple solution is this: shoes, generously given, every time a pair is purchased!

The Ad Council's "Generous Nation" campaign is yet another example of our nation's growing attraction to generosity. How many times have you seen someone who needed help—passed a homeless person on the street, read about a family who lost everything, intended to bring an elderly neighbor a hot meal, or (fill in the blank). But then you got busy or forgot. If you are like most people, lots and lots of times you got busy.

Gary Ginter
(1946–)

GINTER IS a founding partner of Chicago Research and Trading Group, CRT. In 1997, the prospering firm was sold to NationsBank. Ginter still runs the multimillion-dollar futures and options trading unit, which has been dubbed the "envy of the industry." Today he is chairman and CEO of VAST Power Systems and was managing director of Globex. Less well known is Ginter and his wife's yearly channeling of millions of dollars of their fortune to charity and missions. Ginter employs what he calls a "stewardship model": make all he can; live on as little as possible in a simple life-style; and give all the rest away. He started the Jubilee Foundation to structure his giving. The foundation invests in many small mission-related corporations around the world that start real viable businesses. His total giving is estimated at 80 percent of his income.

"Almost Givers"?

The Ad Council's innovative campaign, launched in 2008, is based on the affirmation that America is the most generous society in the world. And when our hearts are touched—as they were by the images we saw after the tsunami and Hurricane Katrina—we gave and volunteered even more. These were fabulous examples of heartfelt generosity. How, some pondered, after the hurricane images faded from the news, could we continue to turn people's best intentions into action day in, day out?

The answer came (pro bono) from a legendary advertising team led by Phil Dusenberry, who headed creative at BBDO for over twenty-five years. He went to his longtime colleagues Ted Sann and Charlie Meismer, and they came up with an idea. When they read the brief, they created a poignant campaign to turn "Almost Givers" into "Givers." The TV spots they created show people in need. The voice-over talks about the people who almost helped. But they didn't. The spots end with the line "Don't Almost Give. Give." When it comes down to it, regardless of motivation, religious impulse, or tradition, it is ultimately about acting, both personally and as a society. True generosity can begin with an emotion or an urge to act, but it does not end there.

The Index of Global Philanthropy, compiled by the Hudson Institute, is a comprehensive annual guide to the sources and magnitude of America's and other countries' charity to the developing world.[7] The U.S. ranks number one in absolute amounts given in 2007 and in the top third of all developed countries measured by Gross National Income. This puts U.S. giving at nearly $300 billion, or three and a half times what the U.S. government gives yearly in foreign aid. These calculations challenge the basis of the OECD's official aid counts, which account only for government-to-government "official development assistance" (ODA). This number has long underestimated the amount and impact of U.S. giving, including private assistance to the developing world. The *Index* finds that in addition to churches, foundations, corporations, charities, and universities, several new players are getting involved in global giving who combine altruism with for-profit business models. Bonds are now issued against small loans to the poor, allowing for private capital flows and growing microfinancial markets. Immigrants are sending more and more money in the form of remittances home to villages and families through customized bank accounts, credit cards, even cell phones. Overall, global philanthropy is growing by leaps and bounds.

GlobalGiving is another excellent example that deserves credit as an innovator at being generous. The online marketplace allows donors to find and fund grassroots projects that appeal to their own specific interests.

GlobalGiving was founded by two former World Bank executives who have created what they believe is "a new, higher-impact way for individuals and organizations to direct their philanthropy to their choice of high-quality, trackable projects in the U.S. and around the world." The GlobalGiving platform aggregates many donations from all types and sizes of donors, creating a new source of reliable funds for project leaders working to improve social, economic, and environmental conditions in their local communities and around the world. It thereby unleashes the potential of people to make positive change happen.

In effect, GlobalGiving has built an efficient, open, thriving marketplace that connects people who discover a community and who have ideas that can change the world with people who can support these ideas. At any given time it offers more than five hundred high-impact grassroots-level projects in over one hundred countries. Project themes range from education and economic development to healthcare and the environment. With nearly

$10 million in donations since 2001, some twelve hundred projects have received funding. Thousands of individual donors and an increasing number of corporations, from Yahoo and Google to PayPal and Gap, are using the platform to extend giving around the globe.[8]

One thing is for certain, as recent research by Havens and Schervish at Boston College's Center on Wealth and Philanthropy documents in a study on millionaires and the millennium: we in the United States are entering a golden age of philanthropy. The next decade or so will witness some $40 trillion passing nationwide from one generation to the next. This is unprecedented in human history. Given recent trends, and the rapid, very impressive rise in philanthropic activity, the future indeed looks bright for giving. Charitable giving is expanding quickly and exponentially. There remain many "what ifs" to resolve (especially after the wealth effects of the present deep recession), but being generous appears to be upon us and increasingly all around us. Thus I am optimistic about the future of generosity, largely because of the emphasis on making sure that our hearts are influenced by our minds. For only if generosity is applied responsibly will it make a true and positive difference in the world.

A Generous Society 8

*There is a wonderful mythical law of nature
that the three things we crave most in life—
happiness, freedom, and peace of mind—are always
attained by giving them to someone else.*

PEYTON MARCH

AN ADMIRER OF Johannes Brahms in his will left the
great German composer one thousand marks. Upon learning of the bequest, Brahms was deeply moved. "It touches
me most deeply and intimately," he wrote to a friend. "All
exterior honors are nothing in comparison." Then, in the
very next sentence, Brahms informed his friend that since
he did not need the money, he was "enjoying it in the most
agreeable manner, by taking pleasure in its distribution."
The very virtue that had touched Brahms inspired replica-
tion of itself in the generosity that Brahms in turn demonstrated. And one can hope and surmise that it stirred
the same virtue among his beneficiaries. Generosity is like
that. It is the virtue that can go on mirroring itself until
the end of time.

Independent Sector, the leading association in the not-for-profit world, examined the relationship between item-izing charitable giving on tax returns and giving levels in contemporary America. You would think that would allow for some very telling comparisons and even a few noteworthy conclusions. According to the data, house-holds that itemize charitable contributions were found to give more than those that did not itemize. No surprise there. Even with tighter IRS rules and stricter documenta-tion requirements, this is expected behavior.

The difference in giving levels is, however, more pro-nounced in the area of religious giving. Itemizers surpass nonitemizers to a greater degree in religious giving than they do in secular giving. In fact, itemizers give nearly two-thirds more to religious causes than nonitemizers.

Clearly there is a relationship between charitable giving and religious conviction. This should not come as a sur-prise, for, as noted earlier, giving begins with an attitude of submission. True givers understand that they are merely managers of their assets. One of the ways they demon-strate their gratitude to God for all that has been done for them is to give with a cheerful spirit.

For some, giving a "tithe" to a church, synagogue, mosque, or some other charity is done not just out of obe-dience or as a grateful response. Many people have come to realize that by giving the first fruits—and by following the biblical principles of thrift and wise management—their material needs are met. Thus, more and more people are choosing to be what could be termed "generous giv-ers" not just to benefit others, but to benefit themselves.

However, many are also discovering that the great-est benefits of a generous life are not practical ones, but spiritual ones. Jesus in Matthew 6:1–4 cautioned against the doing of "alms before men." He said that those who

Andrew Carnegie
(1835–1919)

CARNEGIE BECAME FAMOUS as the U.S. Steel magnate. He believed that personal wealth was not a product of individual intellect or hard work but the result of the opportunities presented in a capitalist democracy. He said every millionaire owes society a debt to be repaid through philanthropy. Carnegie sought to die without a penny left—by giving it all away. By seeking to advance democracy, he funded free public libraries, providing some $56 million over time for 2,509 buildings. He also sought to advance peace-promoting efforts because he saw the ravages of war. Born in Dunfernline, Scotland, Carnegie was the son of a lowly weaver. He came to the United States in 1848 and settled in Allegheny, Pennsylvania. At age thirteen he started working in cotton mills, railroads, and for Western Union. Eventually he organized Carnegie Steel in Pittsburgh, and at the age of sixty-five sold his company to J. P. Morgan for $480 million. He devoted the rest of his life to philanthropic activities and writing. His *Gospel of Wealth* became a classic. In it, he argued that wealth was a trust that is to be administered for the benefit of society. He created seven philanthropic and educational organizations in the U.S. and still more in Europe. He nearly reached his goal and gave away $350 million before he died.

do their alms so that others can see them have already received their reward. The Bible teaches that giving is not a public activity. Only God knows how much of a sacrifice each gift really is. Thus the two mites given by the widow (Luke 21:1–4) were ultimately more in God's eyes than the bags of gold given out of abundance. Be satisfied that God knows what you give and he will certainly reward you in like kind.

This reward, I believe, comes in the form of a deep-seated joy that no amount of money can buy and that only the giver can know. The Apostle Paul spoke of this in reference to the Philippian church that supported his own ministry: "Not that I seek the gift itself, but I seek for the profit which increases to your account" (Phil. 4:17, NASV).

Secular philosophies, too, including that of Kant, recognize that the reward of giving does not consist in some return in the form of reciprocal goods or the approval of bystanders. The reward of giving is the gift itself. And willing, cheerful, unostentatious, and proportionate giving is a source of joy: joy in freedom, in life, and in the overarching presence of the God who is giver of all.

Perhaps the best way to make this point is through a few examples, "case studies," if you will. Dave is a friend of mine. He is wealthy—very wealthy by any earthly measure in terms of financial assets. He has all he needs and more. He is definitely "high net worth," a millionaire many times over. He runs a gold fund and trades in commodities. He was formerly a successful investment banker and serial entrepreneur who started many companies. He took a number of them public. He was once married, but has long been divorced. He has no children or siblings and only a distant extended family. He is of Hungarian descent and has lived in New York City most all of his adult life.

Joan Kroc
(1928–2003)

JOAN KROC made the largest ever gift to charity. Her estate, as the heiress of the McDonald's business, created by her late husband, remains one of the largest in the world. She also owned the San Diego Padres baseball team. She gave $1.5 billion in 2003, 75 percent of her $2 billion fortune, to the Salvation Army. The gift was for construction of thirty to fifty recreation and educational facilities across the U.S. Her other gift was to go into an endowment whose earnings will pay half of the operating costs. She has challenged other donors to pay the remainder. She also started an Institute for Peace and Justice at the University of San Diego, a center for the homeless, and an animal shelter, and has made numerous gifts to Notre Dame University. Her giving is coordinated to support Ronald McDonald Children's Charities and Houses. After witnessing the devastating effects of a flood, she spontaneously gave $15 million to help rebuild the towns of Grand Forks, North Dakota and Minnesota.

He went to an Ivy League university, is well read, and quite sophisticated and urbane. He appreciates good food, art, and wine. I like Dave a lot, and play golf with him nearly every week in the winter.

Dave hates Christmas. His family is half Jewish and half Catholic by conversion a century ago, but he has given up on all religion and thinks himself a humanist at best. Dave admits he lacks any real purpose in his life. He loathes Christmas for two profoundly honest reasons. They don't have to do with the robust holiday commercial economy—he rather likes that beneficial effect. First, and foremost, he hates the gifts. He doesn't give them and doesn't want to receive them either. He finds it obscene that people feel required to give something, particularly something of value, to others. And he hates the manger. The idea that some baby born over two thousand years ago is the Son of God, born into a lowly station in a poor place in some colonial backwater of the Roman Empire to an unwed Jewish girl of no significance is just too much for him to cope with, let alone believe. Dave lacks joy in his life. He fully admits it and he feels bad, really low, depressed, for about a month each year, at Christmas. Dave, as you guessed, is not a particularly generous person.

In contrast, I worked with Ted Turner, founder of CNN, in the early 1990s on a large global project. His is a complex ego that jettisoned Bible believing years ago. Nevertheless, he retains some of the zeal of a new convert. He came over time to believe in giving, not based on faith or some formal religion, but as a hope for humankind. He once said, "The greatest book about giving that I've ever read is *A Christmas Carol* by Charles Dickens, about Scrooge and how happy he was when he started doing things to help Tiny Tim's impoverished family." Turner added, "Remember? His whole attitude changed and he was happy."

Is it really more rewarding to give than to receive? How could that be? The world seems to be structured around

Mother Teresa

(1910–97)

THE ALBANIAN Roman Catholic nun founded the Missionaries of Charity in Kolkata, India, and for over forty years ministered to the poor, sick, orphaned, and dying. She became internationally famous as a humanitarian and advocate for the poor and helpless, as she was portrayed in Malcolm Muggeridge's moving 1970 book, *Something Beautiful for God*. She won the Nobel Prize for Peace in 1979. Her mission expanded to 610 sites in 123 countries, with over 4,000 sisters. It included hospitals and homes for people with HIV/AIDS, leprosy, and tuberculosis, as well as orphanages and schools. Following her death in 1997, she was beatified by Pope John Paul II and given the name Blessed Teresa of Calcutta.

Analyzing her deeds and achievements, John Paul II asked: "Where did Mother Teresa find the strength and perseverance to place herself completely at the service of others? She found it in prayer and in the silent contemplation of Jesus Christ, his Holy Face, his Sacred Heart."

In his first encyclical, *Deus Caritas Est*, Benedict XVI mentioned Teresa of Calcutta three times, and he also used her life to clarify one of his main points of the encyclical: "In the example of Blessed Teresa of Calcutta we have a clear illustration of the fact that time devoted to God in prayer not only does not detract from effective and loving service to our neighbor but is in fact the inexhaustible source of that service." *(continues)*

Mother Teresa specified, "It is only by mental prayer and spiritual reading that we can cultivate the gift of prayer."

getting or taking. So how could "giving" be more beneficial? I discussed the science of generosity in chapter 6, but I resort to it again here to strengthen my case. Brain-imaging research is unwrapping what's behind the joy of giving. It appears that our brains have been hard-wired to give. This being the case, being generous is not only a real option, but it may in fact be the human preference. We were made that way and have evolved over millions of years to be givers. Jordan Grofman, chief of the Cognitive Neuroscience Section of the National Institutes of Neurological Disorders and Stroke (NIDS), a division of the National Institutes of Health, says, "You give from the heart and it satisfies your brain." His research backs this claim.

With philanthropy growing over recent decades, a lot of brains must be lighting up. In Toronto, Canada, four thousand people gather each year a few weeks before Christmas for the Joy of Giving concert. St. Paul's Anglican Cathedral combines with dozens of other choirs across the city to raise money for the largest single donation to the Santa Claus Fund. All monies raised as a result go to local children who live in poverty.

Providing for relatives in need comes more naturally for most people than reaching out to strangers. Blood is blood and it seems easier to help your own, or your own kin and kind. Nevertheless, it could be logically argued that it may be worth being kind to people outside the family, as the favor might be reciprocated in the future. But when it comes to anonymous benevolence, directed to causes that, unlike people, can give nothing in return, what could possibly motivate a donor? There is no *quid pro quo*. The answer given by neuroscience is that it feels good. That answer is fine, so far as it goes, but it is one phrased in terms of neurones, hormones, and neurotransmitters—an explanation that makes no mention of the crucial fact, which is *why* it feels good.

It feels good, I would argue, because it is morally right. The pleasure we take in giving is not like the pleasure we take in a shot of whiskey or a sudden ray of sunlight. It is the pleasure that follows from the knowledge of a duty discharged and a good deed done.

This is truly witnessed when an increasing number of givers begin to realize the full "joy of giving." When you first experience it, it takes over and all you want to do is just give and continue giving. People, beginning modestly, start supporting a particular cause that touches their heart. The money wisely given is not "missed" in their personal portfolio. Then, special giving becomes more consistent. Funds are saved for special projects and then joyfully given. People realize that wise charitable giving, instead of being a financial burden, can actually be financially liberating. People want to be responsible in their giving. They want it to have a positive effect. When they see such effect, they are inclined to give even more, sometimes much more.

To the person who asks, "Who, me?" the answer is, "If not you, who else?" Giving is not just a way to help others. It is not merely a process that transfers another person's pain to our own. In fact, in giving we help ourselves. In giving, we demonstrate that it is we who control our possessions, not vice versa. The health of American democratic capitalism advances with the culture of generosity. Social upward mobility and social health improve. The more we advance in generosity the more we advance in happiness and in turn are motivated to increase the good fortune of others.

In short, there are far too few sources of joy in this life. But perhaps the greatest of them all is the joy that comes from simply giving.

Generosity and Purpose in Life

*Money is like manure; it's not worth a thing unless it's
spread around encouraging young things to grow.*

THORNTON WILDER

THORNTON WILDER of course borrowed this line from
Francis Bacon (Essays XV, 1625) who wrote, "Money
is like muck, no good but it be spread." It's a line that
prompts me to ask the deeper question, "What is the best
life a human being can lead?"

Some of the finest minds of Western moral philosophy
over time have addressed this fundamental question of
human existence. Many of the answers were summed up
in a little book titled *Living the Good Life*.[1] In it, Gordon
Graham introduces undergraduate students to the moral
arguments of Plato, Aristotle, Hume, Kant, Kierkegaard,
Nietzsche, Mill, and Sartre in a dialectical manner that
splices historical thought and the pressing concerns of
modern readers by making genuine connections between
the questions that nonphilosophers argue in real life and
the essential academic ones. What gives our lives the most

meaning and value? What should we want out of life? Is the best life a virtuous one or a happy one? Is happiness composed simply of pleasure? Does religion provide the best guide for a fulfilling existence?

The book is in essence an examination of the many and varied responses to the question of what constitutes a good life. No one philosophical answer triumphs; there is a host of replies, a few systematic but most suggestive in one way or another. Truth is, the question of the good life has been around a long time and does not appear to be in any danger of going away any time soon.

I believe that the ability to live the good life includes making a commitment to noticing and appreciating all the good that surrounds us. Oftentimes, as G. K. Chesterton reminded us, we are incapable of enjoying "what is" because we are so used to it that we no longer notice its newness, its wonder. It has become mundane, almost commonplace. But seeing things again and again should not make them any less wondrous or joyous. We should not be abased by our own familiarity of acquaintanceship. There is splendor in the mundane and the ordinary. Rather we should give thanks, participate in the "great thanksgiving" for all things. Instead of anxiety and alienation, we need to perceive all sources of difference and distance as forms of delight that open us to the infinite, because creation itself is a superfluous gift from God to be enjoyed.

In *T. S. Eliot: A Memoir,* a story is told about how T. S. Eliot once took a cab to London's Heathrow airport. The cab driver, as taxi drivers do, struck up a conversation with him. He told Eliot that earlier that same day he had given a cab ride to Bertrand Russell. T. S. Eliot and Bertrand Russell, though one-time friends, became rivals of a sort. Eliot was a renowned poet and writer who had a

Bill and Melinda Gates
(1955– AND 1964–)

BILL GATES founded Microsoft and watched his wealth mushroom during the decades he ran and grew the software company. When Gates was a boy, his mother volunteered often for the United Way and encouraged him to give time and talent to others. In recent years Gates has stepped down as CEO of Microsoft and focused on his foundation. His passion there is for global health and the elimination of poverty. With a thrust for "solving problems," the Gateses' philanthropy faces the challenges of the world boldly and realizes they are global in nature. Over $6 billion has been given to date, with large grants for combating AIDS in Africa and malaria prevention. It is now the largest charitable foundation in the world. Gates has said publicly that his wealth isn't to be accumulated and preserved for its own sake. He plans to leave his two children only $10 million each, and leave the rest of his vast fortune to his charity. Melinda Gates, his wife, is a copartner in the foundation. Last year, Warren Buffett, Gates' friend and the richest man in America, decided to leave his $30-plus-billion fortune to the Gates Foundation, saying it was best positioned to use it wisely. Gates gave $750 million recently for global vaccines and $1 billion to a global scholarship fund to needy minority students. His plan is to give away even larger sums in the years to come.

conversion to Christianity that greatly influenced his writing. Russell, perhaps the best-known philosopher of his time, was an ardent atheist. The cabbie told Eliot about the earlier conversation, which covered philosophy, existentialism, and literature. "And I asked him what it was all about," said the cabbie in his gruff voice. "And what did he say?" asked Eliot. "He couldn't tell me," the cabbie responded. "He didn't know what life was all about."[2]

Russell did not have an answer. Perhaps he was looking too far afield, scanning the distant horizon for something that was in fact sitting right under his nose. For the answer, to me, is obvious. The answer is *giving*. That is what life is all about. Living well has to do with the extent to which we live generously. That is the key that unlocks a life of fullness. My mother often said to me as a child that "being nice and sharing is no more difficult than its opposite." She was right, even if I struggled with this simple truth for a long time.

How do most people usually live? How is the ballast of their lives usually tilted? Most operate according to an opposite formula, thinking that self-preservation and self-satisfaction are the keys to pursuing the "good life." That's what we've been told and taught. In fact it seems odd, perhaps mildly irrational, that those who give away their lives will encounter what life really means: "Give yourself away and you will find yourself." On the face of it, it just does not seem possible.

I have come to a greater understanding and appreciation of the question Jesus asked in the gospel of Matthew (16:26, NIV): "For what will it profit you to gain the whole world and lose your soul?" I believe that this message should be posted on every billboard across America. It's a message that America, indeed the entire world,

Warren Buffett
(1930–)

BORN IN OMAHA, Nebraska, Buffett is perhaps the quintessential American investor. Only lately has he become a large philanthropist. As CEO of Berkshire Hathaway, his net worth is estimated at over $61 billion. He was ranked by *Forbes* magazine as the richest man in the United States. This so-called "Oracle of Omaha" is a value investor who practices personal frugality. He still lives in a small neighborhood house that he purchased in 1958 for $31,500. Buffett was always a giver of about $12 million a year to his foundation. Then in 2006, he announced, rather surprisingly, a plan to give away his entire fortune, with 85 percent going to the Gates Foundation in the form of class B shares in his company, valued at $30.7 billion. This is certainly the largest charitable gift in history. He also plans to give an additional $6.7 billion to the Susan Buffett Foundation and the foundations of his three children. Buffett has strong thoughts on wealth and why it is to be reallocated. He said, "I don't have a problem with guilt about money. . . . My money represents an enormous number of claim checks on society."

needs to hear. "What if we gained the whole world, but lost our soul?" Counterintuitive, to say the least. Those who want to save their life will lose it; and those who lose their lives—who give away themselves—will find life. The joyful life—the fulfilled life—is a life of self-donation.

The virtue of generosity might very well occupy the central place in our purpose for living. In the words of theologian Robert McAfee Brown, we are here to share our bread. How wonderful it is to know the abundance that comes from giving, to experience the prosperity that depends not on how much we have, but on how generously we live and give.

Remember, as discussed earlier, that living the generous life is not just about giving away money. It is first and foremost about how we choose to live. The generous life signifies a person's faith in God's many blessings. It is lived out of deep thanks. The generous life is therefore primarily one of *service*—using the gifts and the time and talents we have been given to serve others. This is the way to live generously. Such a life takes commitment, time, and practice. It is not achieved all at once, but is pursued over years and decades.

The literary genius C. S. Lewis discusses generosity in *Mere Christianity*. He writes in the chapter "Social Morality":

> In the passage where the New Testament says that every one must work, it gives as a reason "in order that he may have something to give to those in need." Charity giving to the poor is an essential part of morality: in the frightening parable of the sheep and the goats it seems to be the point on which everything turns. Some people nowadays say that charity ought to be unnecessary and that instead of giving to the poor we ought to be producing a society in which there were no poor to give to. They may be quite right

Oprah Winfrey
(1954–)

OPRAH IS an entrepreneur, educator, producer, talk show host, and now a leading philanthropist. After a difficult childhood growing up poor in Mississippi, she became determined to make a better life for herself and others. She is the first black woman to have a nationally syndicated TV show and production company. She is the first black woman billionaire. Today Oprah is one of the most admired Americans of our time. She has both figuratively and literally paved the way for many others and has won dozens of awards, professional and character, to prove it. In 1987 she started her foundation to "support the inspiration, empowerment, and education of women, children, and families around the world." By initiating a national database, she helped launch a campaign against child abuse. She has funded scholarships, built homes through Habitat for Humanity, and encouraged individuals to create "Angel Networks." In 2002 she built a $41 million leadership academy in South Africa for girls. Oprah has made large donations to various historically black colleges and universities. She has said she values financial success as it "enables her to make an important difference in people's lives."

in saying that we ought to produce this kind of society. But if anyone thinks that, as a consequence, you can stop giving in the meantime, then he has parted company with all Christian morality. I do not believe one can settle how much we ought to give. I am afraid the only safe rule is to give more than we can spare.[3]

Measuring Generosity

There are a few indicators that give the world a tangible, visible "report card" on how generously we are living. People cannot claim to say they are living the generous life and not see it reflected in two very tangible things. There are indexes for stock market performance, the S&P 500, the Dow Jones Industrials, and still more indexes to measure other things, including, for example, which countries are most competitive in the global economy. Today we measure almost everything from length to depth to breadth and every hash mark in between. I propose constructing a "Generosity Index" that would chart just two items each along an axis:

- how you use your time (your *date book*); and
- how you use your money (your *check book*)

By calculating these two points along a graph, you could see where you are in terms of generosity. You could tell if you are living a generous life and if any axis is falling short. You could compare yourself with others and against yourself over time, year-to-year, decade-to-decade.

It isn't hard to gauge these two things, painful and transparent as they may be. They reveal a great deal about how one is living life, about what is most important, what

Michael Bloomberg
(1942–)

BORN INTO a Russian Jewish family during World War II in Medford, Massachusetts, Michael Bloomberg is the son of a bookkeeper. He put himself through college at Johns Hopkins and later at Harvard for an MBA.

He joined Salomon Brothers on Wall Street in 1966 and quickly climbed the ladder to become partner and head of equities. In 1981 he left and created his own firm built around financial information and a "specialized computer" that revolutionized the business. Turning next to media, Bloomberg LLP expanded and built an empire.

As one of the wealthiest people in the world (estimated net worth $20 billion), Bloomberg has spent much time and energy on philanthropy. With emphasis on education, medical research, and the arts, he became known as a very generous giver. He has given away over $300 million to his alma mater, Johns Hopkins, alone. He was listed as the seventh largest donor over the last decade in the United States.

In 2001 Bloomberg entered politics and was elected mayor of New York City. He was reelected in 2005. His autobiography, *Bloomberg by Bloomberg*, outlines his life's story and elegantly explains his motivation and strategy on giving. In 2008, he was America's largest giver.

takes first place. They reveal our true priorities. We might deceive ourselves into thinking that no one really sees or takes note of these two items in our index. Perhaps that is true. But how you live your life before God, what you do in private when you are alone, is known. One day we will all be accountable for such doings or not doings, for all our decisions and indecisions, for errors of commission and omission, and for the marks we make on our Generosity Index.

There is a system offered by a company called Make-Good that allows businesses to highlight their positive actions in a third party, standardized format online.

The MakeGood system consists of a badge, profile, and web-based platform. A MakeGood Badge is placed on a businesses' website and symbolizes a commitment to social responsibility. A click on this badge then leads to a MakeGood Profile that displays the positive action a company is undertaking related to social responsibility, such as giving, volunteering, or recycling. The MakeGood Profile includes stories and pictures of how a company is making a difference along with endorsements from the nonprofit that benefits. Lastly, all businesses that are MakeGood members are highlighted at www.makegood.com, where site visitors can search for and see what these companies are doing to make a difference.

The MakeGood system reveals a significant movement in today's giving environment focused on the importance of social responsibility. Companies want to be seen as good corporate citizens. The MakeGood system provides an all-encompassing way of demonstrating corporate social responsibility. It is a way to track and display corporate giving. It is also an all-inclusive approach to giving. Rather than simply supporting one organization to the exclusion of others, the MakeGood metric allows companies to support all forms of giving.

These kinds of developments suggest that the future of generosity is secure and getting more secure each day. Its future becomes more secure as people come to understand generosity not just as an option, but also as a virtue that lies at the very center of the purpose of life.

Final Thoughts 10

*It is every man's obligation to put back into the world
at least the equivalent of what he takes out of it.*

ALBERT EINSTEIN

HABITS, especially "habits of the heart," are observable.
In his *The Principles of Psychology*, written in 1890, William James wrote:

> When we look at living creatures from an outward
> point of view, one of the first things that strike us
> is that they are bundles of habits. In wild animals,
> the usual round of daily behavior seems a necessity
> implanted at birth; in animals domesticated, and
> especially in man, it seems, to a great extent, to be
> the result of education. The habits to which there is
> an innate tendency are called instincts; most persons
> would call some of those due to education acts of reason. It thus appears that habit covers a very large part
> of life, and that one engaged in studying the objective
> manifestations of mind is bound at the very outset to
> define clearly just what its limits are.[1]

The most memorable stories about habitual giving are often those of small children. One of the Rockefeller daughters tells a story that set her giving in motion. At age five she was given fifteen cents weekly as an allowance and she had three boxes in her bedroom. One was marked *expenses*—five cents went there; a second, *savings*—another five cents was put there. And the last was named *charity*, which received the final five cents. This tripartite division was something she learned and tried to stick with her whole life. Giving was a formed habit and it became a way of life. Being generous was instilled as a child and stayed throughout adulthood because it was ingrained early.

Habits are best started young, but what is most important is that they become part of character. The best (and unfortunately the worst) habits become so "habitual" that you don't even realize you are doing them. Born to educators in Chicago, an entrepreneur created the C. D. Moody Construction Company, Inc. Foundation in 1989, only two years after starting his firm, which now posts revenues in excess of $35 million. "I believe you start giving when you have nothing," he says. "Then, when you become successful, it's a habit from the heart. As a businessperson, we have a responsibility to give back to our communities, whether it's time, money or both. Not only because we've been blessed but also because we're role models. We give hope to people."[2]

H. Art Taylor, president of the Better Business Bureau's Wise Giving Alliance, suggests thinking about "problems you want to see solved in society and then identifying organizations working to resolve those challenges." To get into the habit of giving, his organization suggests to include donations in your budget as an expense item, similar to rent or cable services.[3]

The habit of giving touches the heart of every life, and the faithful life especially. Again, it seems to me that I can best make the point by reverting specifically to the religion in which I was raised and to whose wisdom I constantly return for guidance. In Christianity, we are told that life itself is possible because "God so loved the world, that he gave his only begotten Son, that whosoever believeth in him should not perish, but have everlasting life" (John 3:16). Love is at the center of life but giving is the first and most direct result of love. Love of someone is proven in a willingness to sacrifice for that person. It is also expressed in the importance of giving as evidenced when Christ said, "It is more blessed to give than to receive" (Acts 20:35). And, though we tend to measure everything in terms of dollars and cents, the giving referred to is much more than just money. It includes all we are and all we have. It is the primary way in which we acknowledge what we owe to God.

A Formation Process

There is a catchy line in a television commercial for men's suits that rather slyly states, "An educated consumer is our best customer." It's true. Nothing works better than perpetual learning to cement a relationship or to build a habit or good practice. The monasteries were full of what they called "disciplines," which were less physical and more spiritual, including prayers at 3 a.m. every morning. When you talk to profound believers of any religious tradition, or even humanists who think a great deal about the ultimate grounds of human behavior, they all come down to one thing: *formation*.

People need and really seek to be formed—to take shape. Anyone who has a regular regime of exercise or who has

Arthur Blank

(1942–)

 WITH HIS FRIEND and colleague, Bernie Marcus, Blank cofounded Home Depot. He stepped down as chairman when they were the world's largest home improvement retailer. He also owns the Atlanta Falcons football team. He is now dedicated to philanthropic and civic causes. He put $15 million toward the construction of the new Atlanta symphony hall. He plans to give away his wealth during his lifetime. He is focused on entrepreneurship, children's aid, medicine, and Jewish issues. His family foundation's mission is to "promote positive change in people's lives and build and enhance communities where they live." The foundation supports innovative endeavors leading to better circumstances for low-income youth and their families. They have given over $250 million to a variety of charitable organizations.

ever trained for a sport or studied for a big examination knows this well. We apply it in reference to our bodies and our minds. But what about our souls in an era of religious laxity and spiritual searching? Who and what cares for, forms our souls?

"Formation" is an interesting and often employed word used in a wide variety of contexts in every language.

Aerobatics, like the Blue Angels, of course fly in formation. So do geese and ducks. Military units march and deploy in formation. Football players get into formation on both offense and defense on each play before the ball is snapped. Geology has its rock formations and stratum. Governments form coalitions to rule. Even business is conducted according to contract formation in the law. It is not surprising then that all of the world's religious traditions contain elements of religious formation for adherents and those who lead worship. This formation is a kind of nurturance in the experience and practice of personal and social holiness. The goal is a deepening of spiritual awareness, growing in moral sensibility, and building character.

In a culture like ours, where identity is today grounded primarily in what a person "does," ministry is often perceived as a kind of "performance" that requires the acquisition of a body of knowledge, an adequate level of intelligence, several skill sets, and sufficient training to be able to weave all of this together in effective ways. In such an atmosphere, students, young or old, can gain the whole world of knowledge, intelligence, skills, and abilities and still lose their souls. Rarely is ministry perceived as a matter of *being*—being in union with God—from which doing flows. Unless knowledge and intelligence, skill sets and training are grounded in a life of loving union with God for the sake of others, they can be subverted by personal, cultural, social, political, or ecclesial agendas. They can become manipulative, coercive, and even destructive although ostensibly employed in the service of God.

I have talked to a number of leading monks, priests, and professors about formation in Catholic (especially Trappist, Cistercian, Franciscan, and Benedictine) and Protestant (especially Anglican and Wesleyan) traditions. In all of these very different Christian traditions, formation of servants of God requires what is called the imitation of Christ, that is, abandonment to God and to those he loves, or "cruciform living." Such radical abandonment is best accomplished by entering into a spiritual rhythm of being and doing, of resignation and activity.

John Wesley, the eighteenth-century divine, in his own life and ministry, later called Methodism, underscored the value of integration on the way to spiritual maturity. His "conjunctive" theology called for a symbiosis of law and grace, of personal depth and social expression, of developing the life of the mind and that of the soul, and of serving one's neighbor as well as glorifying God as the highest end of life. There are many examples of this same dedication, from the ancient church fathers right through to Mother Teresa and Pope John Paul II. At the very core of this kind of formation is the giving of oneself—which is what "dedication" literally means—and the gratitude that is the reciprocal aspect of that gift.

I am not a priest or a mystic, nor am I trying to make converts to any particular religious dogma. Nevertheless, I would not be doing my subject justice if I left it without offering some aids to the art of giving. In deference to the complexity of any individual life, they are aids that I myself have found useful. But remember that *learning,* like *forming,* is an active verb, one that implies the right state of mind and a perceived need from which the doing emerges.

A Guide to Generosity

Is there a process to generosity? Would such a process, regardless of who we are or where we come from, suggest a more genuine, scientifically based, even universal form of being generous? Such questions are worth considering in the context of the arguments in this book.

What would a "process of being generous" look like? Decisions about giving are like other human decisions. Decision-making is an outcome of a mental process involving cognition leading to selected courses of action(s) producing a final choice. Clearly, all integrated action decisions (like giving) impute a commitment to action. And we would all agree that diagnosis must be properly informed if treatment is to be appropriate. In general, intuitive elements, when combined with informed analysis, will lead to decisions that are both more effective in achieving the goal and more honest in expressing their motive.

However, cognition styles and cultural attitudes differ across societies, even in the more globalized and integrated economy of this twenty-first century. Hence there may be no easy or single way to promote generous living and giving. But here are six techniques that have been used with good result in everyday life to help guide decision-making.

1. List the advantages and disadvantages of any giving option(s).
2. Use random or coincidental methods to demonstrate the effect of acts of kindness.
3. Accept the first option for giving that achieves a desired result.
4. Acquiesce to a known authority or expert and act on that advice for giving.
5. Calculate the expected value or utility of each giving option.
6. Make a decision and follow it through. Then repeat.

In the case of giving, it is the last of those that is most often neglected. It is easy to think that you have succeeded

C. S. Lewis
(1898–1963)

CLIVE STAPLES (KNOWN AS "JACK") LEWIS was born in Belfast, Ireland. He became world renowned as a medieval scholar, Christian apologist, and as a poet and writer of fiction relating the struggle between good and evil. His most famous works, *The Chronicles of Narnia*, have been translated into more than thirty languages and have sold well in excess of a hundred million copies since they were first published in the 1950s. They have been further popularized on stage, TV, and now in cinema.

Jack was a brilliant student at Oxford University, where he won triple "Firsts," the highest academic honor. He went on to teach at Magdalen College, Oxford, for nearly thirty years and later served as professor of medieval and Renaissance literature at Magdalene College in the University of Cambridge.

Lewis was a prolific writer and a jovial soul. He was part of a circle of literary friends known as "The Inklings," which included J. R. R. Tolkien, Charles Williams, Owen Barfield, and Lewis' brother, Warren.

Lewis' own personal example of generosity, while quiet and largely unrecorded, is well worth mentioning in any sincere list of philanthropists. From an early age he was very generous with his money—once when still a schoolboy he was punished for giving money to a beggar at the school gates. When he became a Christian writer, he formed a trust called "The Agape Fund," administered by his lawyer friend,

(continues)

Barfield, into which Lewis paid two-thirds of his royalties. From this fund Lewis gave generously, and nearly always anonymously, to people in need. He typically gave to private individuals who he discovered had particular personal needs rather than to charitable institutions or to causes. The story is told that when a friend heard that Lewis had given money to a beggar in Oxford, the friend remarked that he shouldn't have done so because the beggar would only spend the money on alcoholic drink. Lewis replied, "If I kept the money, I would only have spent it on drink!"

in giving something when you have got rid of the intended gift—say by handing it to some official charity or agency, which may be entirely self-appointed to the role of distributor. But a gift is only a gift when the one in need of it has received it. The case of international aid discussed in a previous chapter reminds us that giving may even worsen the situation of those who need it by increasing the power of their oppressor. Many who gave money to the U.K. charity "War on Want," whose professed aim was to alleviate poverty in the Third World, were distressed to discover that the charity was merely a tool in the hands of Marxist revolutionaries who used the money to advance their goals. And many Muslims have been distressed by similar abuses of the *zakat*, which has too often been appropriated for violent causes with the collaboration of hate-filled mullahs who see no difference between the relief of poverty and armed *jihad*. Such is, indeed, the inevitable danger of any system of giving that has been routinized as a "tithe": and it is one of the themes of this book that tithing and giving are by no means the same idea.

To be generous, therefore, it is not sufficient to give money: you must also give time and energy—the time needed to follow things through and the energy needed to convey your gift into the hands of the ones whom you wish to help. Rather than give your money to an aid agency, why not join with your neighbors in a project of your own? Travel to the place where your help is needed; work out how to establish a school or hospital; raise the funds; set up the network of support. And then enjoy the prospect of success as the initiative grows before your eyes.

I challenge you to consider with greater urgency this virtue of generosity and what it means to your life. Think about its potential to bring hope and comfort to others and joy to your own life. Consider that it might just lie at the center of the very purpose for which we have been created. May you find peace and fulfillment on your journey.

Appendix A
Twenty-one Books to Read on Generosity

Here are twenty-one books arranged by category that will help you and yours on the path to being generous.

For Children

Louise Carus, *The Real St. Nicholas: Tales of Generosity* (Wheaton, Ill.: Quest Books, 2002).

Jean Giono, *The Man Who Planted Trees: Generosity of Spirit as a Source of Happiness* (North Ferrisburgh, Vt.: Heron Dance Press, 2007).

On Art

Ted Purves, *What We Want Is Free: Generosity and Exchange in Recent Art* (Albany: State University of NY Press, 2005).

Jean Starobinski, *Largesse* (Chicago: University of Chicago Press, 1997).

On Thrift

John M. Templeton Jr., *Thrift and Generosity: The Joy of Giving* (Philadelphia: Templeton Foundation Press, 2004).

On Philosophy and Ethics

Jean Bethke Elshtain, *Who Are We?* (Grand Rapids, Mich.: Eerdmans, 2000).

William J. Jackson, *The Wisdom of Generosity: A Reader in American Philosophy* (Waco, Tex.: Baylor University Press, 2008).

Alan D. Schrift, *The Logic of the Gift: Toward an Ethic of Generosity* (New York: Routledge, 1997).

On Economics

Michael Watts, ed., *The Literary Book of Economics* (Wilmington, Del.: ISI Books, 2002).

On Faith

Michael Powell, *A Thousand Paths to Generosity* (London: Spruce, 2004).

Mark Vincent, *A Christian View of Money: Celebrating God's Generosity* (Eugene, Ore.: Wipf and Stock, 2006).

On Motivation and Psychology

Ken Blanchard, *Generosity Factor* (Grand Rapids, Mich.: Zondervan, 2002).

William Kitteredge, *The Nature of Generosity* (New York: Vintage, 2005).

M. J. Ryan and Sylvie Boorstein, *The Giving Heart* (Newburyport, Mass.: Conari Press, 2000).

On Business

Richard John Neuhaus, *Doing Well and Doing Good* (New York: Doubleday, 1992).

On Finances

Ken Rouse, *Putting Money in Its Place* (Boston: New England Financial Advisors, 1996).

On Practical Advice

Claire Guadiani, *Generosity Rules* (Bloomington, Ind.: iUniverse, 2007).

Stephen Slaughter, *Generosity* (Brighton, East Sussex, U.K.: Book Guild, 2002).

On Philanthropy

Arthur Brooks, *Who Really Cares: America's Charity Divide* (New York: Basic Books, 2006).

Giving USA 2007 (annual) (Indianapolis: Indiana University Center on Philanthropy, 2007).

Stanley Katz et al., eds., *Philanthropy and the World's Traditions* (Bloomington: Indiana University Press, 1997).

Appendix B
Real Life Stories of Giving to GlobalGiving

Hinna Mansoor (Ramadan Giving)
Fort Worth, TX

Hinna Mansoor donated to projects on GlobalGiving during the month of Ramadan. She feels that brings out the best in her. Through prayer, she feels close to God and wants to give to others less fortunate. She says, "When I have food and all the blessings, especially in the month of Ramadan, it makes me want to help others who don't have as much."

For Hinna, Ramadan is a way to take time to reflect on being a good Muslim. And that part of being a good Muslim is giving back to others. Since she is from Pakistan, she chose two GlobalGiving projects that involved helping children in Pakistan. "I wanted to give back to my country," she says. Hinna searched the Web to find a charity to give to and "was blown away by the GlobalGiving website." She had a really great experience using Global-Giving. "It was so easy!" Hinna has been busy with her job the whole year and Ramadan gave her a chance to slow down and reflect on things important to her. Giving to others is one of Hinna's priorities and she thanks Global-Giving for allowing her to do this.

Paula Diley
Durham, NC

Paula was raised to be a "giver"—she comes from a family of nine and learned how to share at an early age. Through her siblings, she saw the importance of celebrating with others when they are blessed. Paula feels God has blessed her in so many ways and wants to share, as she is able. This is why Paula has set out a goal to give to all one hundred and ninety-four nations of the world.

Paula's original inspiration came from her pastor who told her "your life will touch nations." She began wanting to "plant seed" in the nations where the different pastors of her church were born. Her first loan was in Ghana, the home of her senior pastor. Paula's pastor has traveled to approximately one hundred and ten countries and she originally wanted to give money to all one hundred and ten. "But then I thought, I could 'plant seeds' in all the nations of the world," she said. If she wanted to continue her giving goals, Paula knew she had to do some more research. This is when she came across GlobalGiving.com.

Now, each time Paula is paid (she works full-time at a ministry and at Michael's arts and crafts store), she first pays her tithes and offerings to her home church, and then searches for projects on GlobalGiving to plant her seed. Her selection process comes as a result of prayer and the search for countries she has not yet given to. Paula maintains a running list of all the countries of the world and crosses each one off as she is able to give. So far, Paula is up to sixty-nine projects in sixty-seven nations! She also makes sure to support a variety of different projects, from play pumps in one country to healthcare issues, water quality, education, schools, economic development, and AIDS awareness. "I started with one project. Giving is very contagious," she says.

One of her giving inspirations is Muhammad Yunus, an economist from Bangladesh. Yunus is a Nobel Peace Prize winner known for his work in microcredit loans. "Muhammad started with a small amount of his own money, and it spread to so many people," Paula says. After she read Muhammad's book *Banker to the Poor*, Paula realized, "I can start exactly where I am and although I only have a small amount to give, combined with others, needs can be met all over the world."

"It is my heart for God and for his people that causes me to give," Paula says. "Every time I give to a project, I get so much joy. It is more blessed to give than receive." If she could give advice to the next generation of young givers, Paula says, "The world is larger than ourselves. Begin with what you have. Giving starts with one."

John Burg and Heather Haines
Washington, DC

Instead of asking for traditional wedding gift items like a blender or toaster, Heather Haines and John Burg decided to register on GlobalGiving.com. "We've been so fortunate, it made sense to be able to give back," Heather explained. "In the spirit of giving, we wanted to be able to give our guests another option." In particular, Heather and John chose three projects for their guests to fund: A library for fifteen hundred students in Mprumem, Ghana; giving microcredit loans to women in Bosnia; and providing bicycles for poor students in India.

All three projects have a unique significance to both Heather and John. The couple is especially excited about the project in India, the destination of their honeymoon. This project is also special since John has been involved in a variety of bicycle projects from Phoenix to West Africa. In addition to putting the India project on their registry, Heather and John are making a contribution of their own in honor of their guests. Plus, there will be bicycle cookies at each table setting!

Already, the response from guests has been incredible, with some already donating on the website. Heather is originally from Texas and went to school in Oklahoma. She says, "It's nice to introduce my friends and family back home to GlobalGiving and see them get excited about it."

Deborah Alley
West Sacramento, CA

For the holiday season, Deborah and her husband purchased GlobalGiving gift cards for each of their nieces and nephews. Deborah felt that her family was so fortunate to have many blessings in life and wanted to give back in a special way. "I want to encourage the next generation of Alleys to think about the world in which they live," she said. Deborah was happy to see that each of her nieces and nephews enjoyed the gift.

Timothy Campbell
New Delhi, India

Tim Campbell is a habitual GlobalGiving gift card buyer!

He explained how his family has always enjoyed the tradition of giving each other donations as well as gifts. He says, "I have recently begun to feel that it is more important to a lot of people I know to be able to support a cause they believe in rather than to receive a physical gift." Tim says he appreciates the fact that GlobalGiving allows people to make a charitable gift to somebody while allowing them to choose the cause, and perhaps find a new project or organization in need.

Tim has given GlobalGiving gift cards to his parents, sister, father-in-law, three brothers-in-law, and several friends. He says, "I have had positive feedback from everyone!"

Tim's current home is in India. He explained how every day he sees the need for social change as well as great work being done by NGOs. He says, "After traveling to Ladakh in the spring, I came home to New Delhi wanting to give something back to a community of people who had been so welcoming to me, yet needed so much in terms of education and opportunity." Tim was able to use GlobalGiving to find an organization that supported primary education in Ladakh based in Delhi, and encouraged friends and family to use the site to donate.

Nicole Shampaine
Washington, DC

Nicole met Dennis Whittle, cofounder of GlobalGiving, and was inspired by the idea of giving to others in need through an online marketplace. When she heard about

GlobalGiving gift cards, she was excited about spreading the word to her friends and family. "I like the idea of giving recipients the option to choose the project they would like to support, instead of picking something for them." GlobalGiving has something for everyone, with projects ranging from environmental issues to bringing poor girls out of poverty through soccer. Nicole says, "I am passionate about almost any type of project!"

The response Nicole got from the GlobalGiving gift cards was amazing. "I gave the gift cards to each of my employees and they absolutely loved them!" Nicole mentioned that she also sent her own family members gift cards for their birthdays and they enjoyed them as well.

Guy Pfeffermann
Washington, DC

Guy Pfeffermann is a longtime friend and supporter of GlobalGiving. Guy goes back to Dennis and Mari's World Bank days: he worked on Russia's country risk analysis with Mari and conducted interviews with companies in developing countries with Dennis. When GlobalGiving first started up, Guy was part of the team as a board member. He says, "I liked the concept. I liked the idea. I was inspired by the energy and enthusiasm."

Since then, Guy has gone on to start his own NGO, Management Education & Research Consortium (MERC), which helps to give students in Africa a chance to succeed in business. The organization finds management schools in Africa and nurtures them. Guy explains, "Have you seen that show *Fawlty Tower* on BBC? It's about a seaside hotel that is run horribly, nothing works, and it's incredibly dysfunctional." He continues, "Think of a country where everything is run like *Fawlty Towers*. Is that going to help the poor?"

The MERC team uses a networking approach to connect the top business schools in the Western world to those in Africa. The schools engage in cooperative programs and receive high-quality training in teaching. "It's a win-win situation," Guy says: "The foreign professors learn just as much as the African professors." MERC is currently working with over thirty-two mentoring schools and seventeen African schools. He says with a smile, "It's the first time there has been a quality benchmark for higher education in Africa."

Guy's path to development hasn't always been straightforward. He says, "When I finished high school, I had no idea what I wanted to do." Guy eventually decided to get into law and economics and enrolled at the University of Paris. He soon came to realize that "law was not his thing," and he didn't see a place in learning about advanced country economics. Instead, he focused on his social life, grinning, "I had such a good time at the student hostel in Paris that I almost flunked my final exams!" There was one class on development economics, however, that really caught Guy's attention. "I had a professor that made things interesting. He got us to read, which was uncommon in France at the time." This is when Guy discovered developing countries.

The list of Guy's work and travel experience is impressive, with time spent in countries ranging from Senegal to Argentina and as a chief economist at the World Bank. He says, "Don't laugh, but some of my inspiration comes from comic strips. I grew up reading *Tin Tin*. It put me in my own mental universe. Things were interesting, exotic, exciting. I wanted that in my job."

When asked about his view on the prospects of achieving the Millennium Development Goal of ending world poverty in his lifetime, he says, "A lot of people have been lifted out of poverty. The solution isn't going to come from aid, it's going to come from markets." Guy is one of the top donors to the GlobalGiving market. Why does he give to GlobalGiving and in his work? "What else do you do in life? If I didn't believe in it, I wouldn't do it. Giving is deeply fulfilling."

Shalom Flank
Washington, DC

Every year at Chanukah, Shalom Flank sits down with his nieces to pick a project on GlobalGiving. He says, "It opens up discussions on different problems in the world and what it means to help others." But Shalom's commitment to give doesn't just stop during the holiday season. In his daily life, he follows traditional Jewish practices where *tzedakah*—acts of righteousness or charity—play an important role. Shalom practices both custom and Jewish law, which call for *tzedakah* at daily prayer, at the time of a *yahrtzeit* (the anniversary of someone's death), and on holidays both joyous and somber.

Shalom views *tzedakah* as a *mitzvah*, often translated as a "commandment" or a religious precept. He tells of an ancient Jewish text that emphasizes how the reward of one *mitzvah* is to be led to the next *mitzvah*. He says, "When I find the right project on GlobalGiving, I have a feeling of connection where I know it's possible to make a real difference." Shalom continues, "That positive feeling is not only its own reward, but also leads to more such acts."

The ability to connect with a project, knowing that his

donation is making an impact is something important to Shalom. On GlobalGiving, he says, "Giving *tzedakah* doesn't just feel like a passive salve for some of the world's terrible sores. It's more like active participation, in real acts of righteousness and justice." The feeling of engagement in helping to solve some of the world's toughest problems flows into other spheres of Shalom's life, enriching his family and communal life.

According to Jewish law, it is preferable that both the recipient of *tzedakah* and the donor remain anonymous. This approach helps to avoid a sense of dependence for those taking *tzedakah*, and reduces a sense of superiority for those who are giving. The GlobalGiving website reminds Shalom of the Talmudic *kuppah*, the anonymous fund the rabbis invented to raise enough *tzedakah* to support community projects. He says, "GlobalGiving strikes an ideal balance in Jewish theories of the 'perfect charity.'" Perhaps the most important thing, however, is that "the projects are almost always created from the bottom-up by social entrepreneurs in their own communities." Shalom says, "These projects are such well-formulated steps to self-reliance, it's a privilege to be able to lend a hand and a *mitzvah* too."

Appendix C
About GlobalGiving

GLOBALGIVING (www.globalgiving.com) is the leading Internet-based network for peer-to-peer philanthropy. Its mission is to sustain a high-powered "marketplace for good" that connects donors directly to the causes they care most about. Through GlobalGiving, individuals and corporations can maximize the impact of every dollar by efficiently and transparently directing their donations to projects here at home and around the world. Since its launch in 2002, GlobalGiving has helped thousands of donors give over $15 million to approximately one thousand projects worldwide. GlobalGiving is based in Washington, DC.

Notes

INTRODUCTION

1. Nicholas Negroponte, *Being Digital* (New York: Vintage, 1996).
2. Adam Smith, *The Theory of Moral Sentiments* (London: FQ Classics, 2007), 219.

CHAPTER 3 *Stewardship Spirituality*

1. John H. Gurney, "Fair Waved the Golden Corn," in *Marylebone Collection*, 1851.
2. Alexis de Tocqueville, *Democracy in America*, 2 vols., 1835, 1840.
3. David Riesman, *The Lonely Crowd* (New Haven, CT: Yale University Press, 1950).
4. United States Council of Catholic Bishops, *Stewardship: A Disciple's Response* (Washington, DC: United States Conference of Bishops, 1993), 24.

CHAPTER 4 *Time, Treasure, and Talent*

1. Mordecai Paldid, *Paths of the Righteous* (London: Krav, 1993).
2. *Lord of the Rings: The Fellowship of the Ring*, directed by Peter Jackson (2001).
3. John Calvin, *Institutes of Christian Religion* (Grand Rapids: Eerdmans, 1990) 1: chap. 5.
4. Bernard Mandeville, *The Fable of the Bees: Private Vices, Publick Benefits* (Indianapolis: Hackett, 1997).

CHAPTER 5 *Generosity and Economics*

1. Herb Gintis, *Game Theory Evolving* (Princeton, NJ: Princeton University Press, 2000), 79.
2. Tibor Machan, *Generosity: Virtue in the Civil Society* (Washington, DC: Cato, 1998).
3. Abraham Kuyper, "Sphere Sovereignty," in *Lectures on Calvinism* (New York: Cosimo, 2007).
4. Arthur Brooks, *Who Really Cares: America's Charity Divide, Who Gives, Who Doesn't and Why It Matters* (New York: Basic Books, 2006), 56.

CHAPTER 6 *Generosity and Science*

1. See Paul Zak, *Moral Markets* (Princeton, NJ: Princeton University Press, 2007), xviii, and various articles in *Scientific American*.
2. Martin Nowak, *Evolutionary Dynamics* (New York: Belknap, 2006).
3. Frans de Waal, *Primates and Philosophers* (Princeton, NJ: Princeton University Press, 2006).
4. Stephen Post, *Why Good Things Happen to Good People: The Exciting New Research That Proves the Link Between Doing Good and Living a Longer, Healthier, Happier Life* (New York: Broadway, 2008).

CHAPTER 7 *Responsible Generosity*

1. William Easterly, *The White Man's Burden* (New York: Penguin, 2007).
2. Andrew Wallis, *Silent Accomplice* (Paris: Tauris, 2007).
3. Michael Maren, *The Road to Hell* (New York: Free Press, 2002).
4. Gurcharan Das, *India Unbound* (New York: Anchor, 2002).
5. Barbara Metzler, *Passionaries: Turning Compassion into Action* (West Conshohocken, PA: Templeton Foundation Press, 2006).
6. Marc Freedman, *Encore: Finding Work That Matters in the Second Half of Life* (New York: Public Affairs, 2008).
7. Center for Global Prosperity, *The Index of Global Philanthropy* (Washington, DC: Hudson Institute, 2008), 6–7.
8. http://www.globalgiving.org.

Chapter 9 *Generosity and Purpose in Life*

1. Gordon Graham, *Living the Good Life* (New York: Paragon, 1990).
2. Joseph Chiari, *T. S. Eliot: A Memoir* (London: Enitharam Press, 1982), 26.
3. C. S. Lewis, "Social Morality," in Lesley Walmsley, ed., *C. S. Lewis Essay Collection and Other Short Pieces* (London: HarperCollins, 2000).

Chapter 10 *Final Thoughts*

1. William James, *The Principles of Psychology* (New York: Cosimo, 2007), 104–6.
2. C. D. Moody Construction, "About Us," http://www.cdmoody construction.com/about_cdmoody.html.
3. Better Business Bureau, http://www.bbb.org/us/.

Photograph Credits

Johann Sebastian Bach courtesy of Jupiter Images Unlimited

Arthur Blank courtesy of Getty Images Sports; photographer
Paul Spinelli

Michael Bloomberg courtesy of the Office of the Mayor,
The City of New York

Warren Buffett courtesy of the Bill & Melinda Gates
Foundation

Henry Ford courtesy of the Collections of The Henry Ford

George Cadbury courtesy of Jupiter Images Unlimited

Andrew Carnegie courtesy of Jupiter Images Unlimited

Bill & Melinda Gates courtesy of the Bill & Melinda
Gates Foundation

Gary Ginter courtesy of Gary Ginter

Calouste Gulbenkian courtesy of the Calouste
Gulbenkian Foundation

Li Ka-shing courtesy of the Li Ka-shing Foundation

Sebastian Kresge courtesy of The Kresge Foundation

Joan Kroc courtesy of Luce, Forward, Hamilton,
& Scripps LLP

C. S. Lewis courtesy of the Marion E. Wade Center

Eli Lilly courtesy of Eli Lilly and Company

The Maclellan Family courtesy of the Maclellan Family Foundations

Felix Mendelssohn courtesy of Jupiter Images Unlimited

Mother Teresa courtesy of the Mother Teresa Center

J. C. Penney courtesy of Getty Images (Hulton Archives); photographer Pictorial Parade Staff

Joseph N. Pew Jr. courtesy of Temple University Libraries Urban Archives

John Rockefeller courtesy of the Rockefeller Archive Center

Wafic Rida Saïd courtesy of www.waficsaid.com

Jeffrey Skoll courtesy of the Skoll Foundation

John Walton courtesy of Weber Shandwick

William Wilberforce courtesy of Jupiter Images Unlimited

Oprah Winfrey courtesy of Getty Images (WireImages); photographer Steve Granitz

About the Author

THEODORE ROOSEVELT MALLOCH has since its inception been chairman and chief executive officer of The Roosevelt Group, a leading strategic advisory and thought leadership company. He is also the founder and chairman of the not-for-profit Spiritual Enterprise Institute (SEI), created in 2005.

In 1994 he cofounded and has since directed the CEO Learning Partnership for PricewaterhouseCoopers LLP. Ted has been a senior fellow and vice president of The Aspen Institute, where he previously directed all of its national seminars and ran the Wye River Conference Centers. He was also president of the World Economic Development Congress sponsored by CNN, "The common frame of reference for the world's power elite." That congress focused on "Building the Integrated Global Economy" and offered some twenty-five hundred chief executive officers, ministers of government, and investment and economic leaders from around the world a forum where new business relationships were established. At that meeting, Margaret Thatcher, the congress chairperson, called him "a global sherpa."

Dr. Malloch has served on the executive board of the

World Economic Forum, which hosts the renowned Davos annual meeting in Switzerland. He held an ambassadorial level position as deputy executive secretary in the United Nations in Geneva, Switzerland (1988–91), where EDI was founded; he headed consulting at Wharton-Chase Econometrics; has worked in international capital markets at the investment bank, Salomon Brothers, Inc.; and has served in senior policy positions at the U.S. Senate Committee on Foreign Relations and in the U.S. State Department. He has taught and lectured at a number of universities in the U.S., Canada, and abroad.

Ted earned his PhD in international political economy from the University of Toronto, where he held the Hart House Open University Fellowship. He took an MLitt degree (honors) from Aberdeen University in Scotland on a St. Andrews Fellowship and earned a BA from Gordon College. He was awarded an honorary LLD degree from the University of Aberdeen in 2008 for his contribution to civil society. He is a research professor at the Claremont Graduate University and Drucker School of Management and at Yale University. He has authored seven books: *Beyond Reductionism* (Irvington, 1982); *Trade and Development Policy* (Praeger, 1989); and along with Don Norris, *Unleashing the Power of Perpetual Learning* (1998); *The Global Century* (NDU, 2001); *Renewing American Culture: The Pursuit of Happiness*, with Scott Massey (M&M Scrivener, 2006); *Spiritual Enterprise: Doing Virtuous Business* (Encounter, 2008); and *Thrift: Rebirth of a Forgotten Virtue*, forthcoming 2009; numerous journal articles, corporate and governmental reports, and has appeared frequently on television and Web casts and as a keynote speaker.

He serves on numerous corporate and mutual fund and not-for-profit/educational boards, including The Templeton Foundation, Yale Divinity School, and the University of Toronto International Governing Council. He advises numerous international and U.S. governmental advisory bodies. He recently went on the board of advisors of GlobalGiving.